From Machismo To Mutuality

FROM MACHISMO
TO
MUTUALITY

Essays on
Sexism and Woman-Man Liberation

by
Eugene C. Bianchi
and
Rosemary R. Ruether

PAULIST PRESS
New York / Paramus N.J. / Toronto

Cover Design: Dan Pezza

Library of Congress
Catalog Card Number: 75-25443

ISBN: 0-8091-0202-1

Published by Paulist Press
Editorial Office: 1865 Broadway, N.Y., N.Y. 10023
Business Office: 400 Sette Drive, Paramus, N.J. 07652

Printed and bound in the
United States of America

TABLE OF CONTENTS

Introduction

Eugene C. Bianchi

Cultural critics have frequently pointed out that America is a land of fads. I can attest to this social phenomenon in a personal way during the past four decades of my life. I have witnessed dress styles, musical tastes and manner of speech come and go in flurries. A charismatic politician or a rock music star will stir up millions of fervent devotees. Movements also have their moments on this rapidly shifting stage: ecological, civil rights and anti-war. Certainly the last have not lost the significance of their central messages, although popular enthusiasm for them has waned. While there is an element of faddism in even the most important movements, opponents of such causes usually seek to dismiss all of them. In the last few years this has been the fate of the feminist movement, the subject around which the following eight essays have been written. "Women's lib" is the tidy expression that packages and controls a fascinating though peripheral development of the 1960s for those who use that terminology.

The chief message of this book is that the movement for female-male liberation in its central insights and convictions is in no way a fad. On the contrary the new awareness and activity against sexism in our culture constitute a probe to the underlying core of oppression that also manifests itself in totalitarianism, racism and militarism. These destructive ideologies stem in many ways from the primordial distortions of how men and women understand themselves and relate to one another; for all of these "isms" are predicated on the estrangement and demeaning of one group for the sake of power and self-identity of the dominant group. The primal symbol of this human condition is patriarchy, which consists in the alienation and suppression of women as a subservient category to a twisted view of masculinity.

Patriarchy is so deeply entrenched in social institutions, East and West, that we tend to accept it as an immutable axiom of nature and divinity. A passage from the ancient Hindu scripture *Manu-Smrti* clearly manifests patriarchal sexism in Eastern antiquity: "In childhood a female must be subject to her father, in youth to her husband; when her lord is dead, to her sons; a woman must never be independent." The same doctrine was announced in the formative period of our republic. In May 1776 John Adams, responding to his wife Abigail's call for legal rights for women, wrote: "We know better than to repeal our masculine systems."

Nearly two millennia separate these quotations, but the Hindu legalist and the American statesman were of the same mind. It is interesting to reflect that during that brief period of gestation of the republic's constitutional framework, the rights of women—as well as those of slaves—had a slim but actual chance of being written into our laws. But the expectations and seeming self-interest of patriarchy were too powerful to be mitigated. When this volume appears it will be nearly two hundred years since John Adams penned those words to his wife. As we celebrate our nation's bicentennial we could profit by personal and social pondering on the roots of sexism that entangle the American dream of a just and caring community and choke off its promise.

Professor Ruether and I approach our task in these essays as theologians whose previous writing and teaching has focused on cultural and political developments in the modern world. As persons who have explored spiritual dimensions of our heritage, we will bring in a number of religious themes. But religion as we understand it is not confined to the boundaries of ecclesiastical institutions. In a more profound and universal way religious myth and symbol has been a powerful language for expressing the dilemmas of human life. The great religious myths and images of history are not mainly tales and signs about another world, but rather they form empowering ways of bringing to awareness the experiential brokenness and hope of our personal and social predicament. Theological language therefore is intimately linked to the motivating spirit and worldviews by which as individuals and nations we think, decide and act. Understood correctly, religious language is neither parochial nor the monopoly of a particular group. In the context of our topic we will translate some of the master images of traditional theology into the meanings of sexism and seek a resolution.

Although Rosemary Ruether and I deal with sexism in America from a similar theological perspective, she and I differ on content and method. She brings to her discussions an expertise in historical theology.

This places the whole question against the broad horizon of Western churchly and secular civilization. She makes us aware that the issues are not of recent vintage, and she indicates the vast changes of mentality and structure needed to create a new man-woman environment. She also examines topics from the experiential stance of a woman in this culture. In a complementary way I have tried to approach the material from the standpoint of the development of the male psyche, a subject that has received relatively little attention in contemporary feminist literature. Two of my essays concern the formation of men by dealing with the experiences of my own history. Autobiography puts our little stories within the optic of the large cultural topics that Professor Ruether elaborates. Furthermore, we have formulated a few reflection and discussion questions at the end of each chapter in the hope that the queries arising from both history and cultural theology can be personalized by readers. In general, we have tried to be conscious of complementarity in content and method in our respective pieces. The desire to complement pervaded our thinking from January 1974 when we set about preparing some of this material for joint delivery at Hanover College in Indiana in the late spring of the same year.

In the first chapter Ruether paints a panoramic vision of sexism in Western culture and theology on a broad historical canvas. Implicit in this treatment is the view that we cannot understand and alter the psychic and societal patterns of our time unless we grasp the breadth and depth of the problem. Few people realize how much the status of women has been linked to considerations of private property; even fewer appreciate how thoroughly the economic and social misogynist mind has projected women into the zone of evil.

I follow this discussion with an autobiographical piece that attempts to put the historical into a self-story. Can we understand the tale of Western history in the microcosm of our own life experiences? The more we can transfer the large issues of history and viewpoint on sexism to our own lives, the more difficult it becomes to view the challenges as academic issues. If I can see and question the previous of my finite existence I can begin to foresee the kind of man I may yet be. This reflection also made me conscious of the incompatibility between patriarchal attitudes and authentic religious faith.

Ruether narrows the focus of her historical searchlight on to the 19th century matrix of our current problems of sexism in America in

Chapter Three. The cult of true womanhood as we have known it in our lifetimes is intimately related to changes in the structure of family life and of childhood in industrialized society. The cleavage between church and world has become in technological society the rift between a privatized world of home morality and the amoral, secular arena of public life. This important historical shift provides an indispensable perspective for understanding feminine subordination and repression in the United States today. I use Chapter Four to explore violence, personal and social, in the context of the industrialized, imperial nation described by Ruether. While violence is an overriding concern in this nation, its relationship to the formation of the male psyche is usually neglected. From boyhood to manhood the American male is conditioned by various social institutions to seek self-meaning and status by means of aggression. In the man's world the violence we associate with crime represents only the tip of the iceberg of aggression that permeates economic and political life. How is the male mystique with its penchant for violence related to the fundamental ethos of America and to the core spirit of the Judeo-Christian tradition?

In Chapter Five Ruether takes up another important facet of contemporary life, the depersonalization of sex. Against a history of ascetic sexuality and the present situation of libertine permissiveness can we integrate sexual liberation with the liberation of whole persons? Have we overloaded the nuclear family in demanding that it supply all of our affectional needs? If the answer is yes, what kind of creative thinking do we require concerning sexual exclusivity in marriage? Can we sustain family stability and personal growth by cultivating a plurality of friendships among men and women? These questions bear closely on our attitudes about homosexuality, which Ruether places in a new perspective. In Chapter Six, I take up psychic celibacy, which is an underlying condition of the depersonalization of sex throughout our culture. But how can we move away from the all-pervasive atmosphere of psychic celibacy toward a society of mutuality? I argue that our era is better disposed than the past for these new forms of self-understanding and interaction. Both men and women can develop towards wholeness by fostering a balance of personality qualities that previously had been restricted to one sex.

How can the traditional language of Western religion come alive in the experience of contemporary women? Ruether turns her theological acumen to this reinterpretation of symbol in Chapter Seven. Terms such as the fall, original sin, salvation, resurrection and exodus make new sense

when agitated in the crucible of feminine self-consciousness and self-definition. On the personal level, Ruether advocates for women the combination
of self-esteem and indignant protest against oppressive conditions. On the
social plane, she underscores a widespread restructuring of society according to a communitarian-socialist vision. Sisterhood becomes a necessary
step in this process, but it must avoid the perils of an exclusive, feminine
separatism. In the final chapter I return to an autobiographical pursuit of
the path from *machismo* to mutuality. I try to deal with my own experiences and struggles to take small steps toward a community of mutuality.
Home chores, job/money issues, decisions about parenthood and outside
(of marriage) friendships are some of the topics that I have confronted in
recent years. In every field men need to ask themselves what they can do
to create relationships of equality with women for perhaps the first time.
Yet there are also benefits for men in such a development that can mo-
tivate them to want and to implement mutuality. What are the conditions
and possibilities for genuine co-humanity between the sexes and within
each of them?

We hope that these essays, which have grown out of our research,
teaching and personal experience will stimulate reflection and reaction on
the part of readers. We are conscious of the brevity and incompleteness of
our book, although the major points can be sustained by a growing body
of literature. Of more vital concern to us is the significance of the discussion to the approaching American bicentennial year. Nineteen seventy-six
could become an occasion for national self-examination in the light of the
principles that gave birth to the republic. What kind of United States do
we want for ourselves and our children as we enter the nation's third century? Answers to that question will involve the working out of the principles of justice, equality and overarching respect for human dignity that
inspired the best spirits of our founders in the eighteenth century.

In the practical order these general themes will affect problems of
maldistribution and poverty, of hunger and war, of population and ecology. But it is very unlikely that any of these great issues will be adequate-
ly confronted unless we are able to go beyond John Adams' "masculine
systems." For the latter are predicated on an individualistic premise of
self-aggrandizement through the accumulation of power and wealth for a
dominant few. The masculine mystique that now governs America and
the world calls for profound scrutiny. We need to discover again, through
an examination of our roles and attitudes as men and women, that com-

munal impulse and care at the heart of American religion and society. For two hundred years of our national life we have denied equal and full status to women. The Equal Rights Amendment will help to correct this injustice, but the transformation must go deeper than legislation alone. It calls for nothing less than a radical reshaping of our identities as men and women and for new styles of human interaction among us.

Eugene C. Bianchi
Berkeley, California
August 1974

Chapter I

Sexism and Liberation: The Historical Experience

Rosemary Ruether

The symbolic structures of sexism exist in our society and in our psyches like a series of archeological strata that have been laid down on top of each other. These strata can be traced in their historical development in various periods from remote pre-history, whose roots are lost in the mists of time, to changes occurring in both the family and the role of women as a result of industrialization. But these strata also continue to live on as symbolic structures in our consciousnesses and inform our notions of male and female "natures" and social roles. In this introductory essay it would be useful to sketch briefly these strata not only in their context of historical development, but also to see how they function in our present social psychology. In Chapter Two of this collection, Eugene Bianchi will give an autobiographical description of how these symbols are formed in our present cultural consciousness.

Both in our collective historical experience of human cultural evolution, and to some extent repeated in the history of every individual, the mother at first appears all-powerful. The first symbolic power on earth appears to be maternal. All human beings originate from the mother's womb. All living things originate from the womb of nature. Maternal or uroboric language provides the first strata for understanding ontology and survives in that language that speaks of God as "Ground of Being." The prominence of mother nature goddesses in early religion express this early experience of the mother as the foundation of existence. Originally, the mother appears a powerful and autonomous figure, and men seek power

7

by first basing themselves upon her. Then they gradually suppress this symbol into a subordinate status.

This symbolic power of the mother should not be confused with political domination by women. Indeed it appears that even from the first the symbolic power of the mother conflicted with the political subordination of women; but this subordination seems to have been more equalitarian and reciprocal in tribal societies, especially in societies that have not yet developed class stratification. The patriarchal cultures that arose in Hebrew and Greek society in the first millenium before the Christian era make their entrance after a struggle against nature and mother religion and the advent of an increasing misogyny toward women in culture. The mother symbol was denegrated and suppressed. The increasing development of males of the elite class was not matched by a corresponding development in women, instead the women of the leadership class were cut out of education and widening cultural experience and pressed into the narrow enclave of the home. The home, which was once itself the center of public life, the nucleus of society itself, has now become a ghetto within which women were confined. It is in this sense that we can say that civilization arises by suppressing and retarding women and making the mother the symbol of the sphere to be conquered and dominated.

In this sense sexism can be seen as rooted in a world historical "war against the mother" that represents the struggle of the transcendent ego to free itself from bondage to nature. But by making women the symbol of nature, consciousness arose in a onesided and antagonistic way. One half of humanity was not the partner in this evolution, but made the symbol of the enemy to be conquered and dominated. Each generation of daughters was then subjected to the fate of their mothers without being allowed their own rise to consciousness side-by-side with their brothers. The psychodynamics of self-knowledge were spurred by negation rather than cooperation with the "other." Males rose by sacrificing each generation of women to their own children. History became the holocaust of women.

Within patriarchal culture we can distinguish strata of symbolism toward women. The first strata we might call "primary patriarchy." This stage organized male/female relations and family life to society so that women appeared as permanent dependants and the quasi-property of patriarchs. By patriarchs we mean "male heads of families," not all males. This kind of society was reflected in the laws of the Old Testament, which are not addressed to women or even to all men. They are addressed solely to the male heads of families, the only public persons in the social and legal sense. Under them were classes of persons who remain permanent dependents. They were not addressed directly by the laws but only as persons to be dealt with by the laws in relation to the ruling males. The "familia" of the patriarch included wives, concubines, children, slaves and cattle. Women were dealt with as quasi-chattel in the sense that various laws dealt with them in terms of the property rights of the patriarch. The transfer of women to another male in marriage, the right to sell them into slavery, the violation of property rights when rape or adultery with a married woman occurred—all this was part of the framework of property rights of husband or father. Women were not just property of course; they were also persons—but dependent persons. As such they were dealt with in terms of their protection and their duties to their lord. Indeed the very word for husband in the Old Testament means essentially one's "lord" and has been assimilated into the language of the relation of the community to God.[1]

Women, as quasi-property and permanent dependents, could never "grow up" and become autonomous persons within patriarchal society. This affected their economic, social and legal status. Women were not public political persons able either to lead or to represent themselves in political assemblies and courts of law. They could not vote or testify in court, much less be elected to lead or to judge. This appears sometimes to have been violated in hereditary societies where women became monarchs, but essentially women appeared in these roles as place-holders for male heirs. This generally meant that women could not inherit property or hold property autonomously. Their own inheritance or earnings belonged to their husbands. Sometimes a loophole developed in this rule when the paternal family sought to keep its own property intact and prevent it from being alienated through its daughters to the clans of their husbands. It was this loophole that gradually won property rights for Roman women under later Roman law.[2] But the rule was that property was passed between males; father to son and father to husband, with women as dependent go-betweens at most.

This status of women economically, politically, juridically, lasted in Western civilization until the 19th century, when women staged their great civil-rights movement to win for themselves autonomous recognition as public persons: to vote, to inherit and manage property, to represent themselves and to control their own earnings.[3] These rights were won painfully by a struggle that took more than a century and even now many remnants of the patriarchal subordination of women, especially married women, remain. When a married woman who makes a full income is denied a credit card or prevented from making a major purchase in her own name she is suffering from the remains of a legal status that denied to her autonomous economic status. Remnants of laws or practices that treated women as permanent minors under the jurisdiction of fathers or husbands abound in our society, especially in the economic realm. When American jurists looked for justification for slavery in English common law it is not surprising that the analogy on which they built was the legal status of women as permanent minors and chattel.[4] Not only was the status of women similar to slaves, but these two categories had been traditionally linked together in patriarchal law. That is why in the Old Testament passages dealing with the duties of women and those of slaves tend to appear together. But even in the New Testament, passages admonishing wives to obey their husbands appear side-by-side with parallel passages admonishing slaves to obey their masters (I Tim. 2, 9-15 and 6, 1-2. Also Titus 2, 4-5 and 9).

This status of women in patriarchy classically included various exclusions from the means of being enculturated into and participating in public life. This meant not only exclusion from the political franchise but also from sacerdotal roles because the public sacerdotal roles traditionally were linked closely to kingship. The public priesthoods were either fused with that of kingship or set by the side of the king to validate kingly authority. Women could be neither kings nor priests. Insofar as women exercised religious roles they typically were the charismatic roles that were outside the public systems of power: the occasional prophetess, wise woman, soothsayer or witch. The religious gifts of women therefore tend to be pressed into the realm of dangerous subversion of male political sacerdotal power and associated with the demonic. The spiritual power of men was channeled into public priesthood; the spiritual power of women marginalized or villified as witchcraft.[5]

Women were also excluded from public educational institutions. The process by which human history accumulated its own experiences and in turn inculturated the next generation into the memory of that heritage was a process from which women were largely excluded as either teachers or learners. This has been the central means for the exclusion of women both from history and from creative contributions to culture. If one asks why there have been so few feminine contributions to culture, one does not have to go much further than this to find the cause. This means that the experiences of women did not become a part of the public record of culture. This continued to be true even when women began to break into history and to create changes that are properly historical. The women's movement of the 19th century created decisive changes in the millenia-old political, legal and social role of women, and yet this story is normally ignored in male-written history books and courses. Only with the new surge of women in universities and society is this story being revealed; yet it is doubtful that it is taught much outside of special courses on women.

In Jewish society the highest destiny of human life was the study of Torah. The rabbinical scholar was the most revered person in the community and the purpose of human life itself was located in the study of Torah; but women were not called to its study. The best a woman could do was to send her sons to study and to create a household that allowed her husband to study Torah. Jewish custom even allowed a woman to undertake the economic support of the family if it freed her husband or son to study. She was clearly a second-grade and auxiliary being within the values of human development.[6] In Christian society, the university was a creation of the Church. The cleric and the scholar were one and the same (as is evident both from our language, where the word "clerical" still has both meanings.) The scholar originally was a celibate in minor orders. Women could be neither clerics nor scholars at medieval universities. It is true that the women's religious order offered women some education but it was primarily in the realm of pious reading and hymn singing. They were excluded from the great structures of academic life.

Women often found ways to circumvent this exclusion, especially in the Renaissance when libraries were accumulated at home and primary education was offered in privacy. In this way a group of educated women arose in the upper class. But their cultural productions remain marginal and mostly in the realm of the private genres of love poetry or personal feelings. They were seldom able to interact with the great structures of higher education that trained men for roles of power.[7] I suspect that the prevailing assumption that women are more intuitive than men derives largely from this marginalized situation. Almost deprived of the tools for really knowing and being able to articulate the larger structures of the world, women have had to rely on their wits to fill in the gaps of their knowledge. Like the blinded person whose ears become very acute, women deprived of knowledge had to guess at the forces that shaped their lives. Men therefore praised them for their intuition or villified them for their emptiness and stupidity.

This exclusion of women from education with all its consequences has lasted until recent times. The goals of the first women's movement in the 19th century were the vote and the university, the overcoming of the two expressions of patriarchy: the status of women as dependents and their exclusion from education. Again remnants still persist both in the continuing exclusion of women from the public record of culture and the marginalization of women within the educational process. Although women start out as equals in education and even a jump or two ahead of their brothers on the grade school level, by high school they are already being taught in subliminal ways that the marriageable girl is one who hides her brains. By the time we reach the tenured professors of universities, the presence of women has been reduced to about one percent. Women in universities have only begun to address themselves to the fact that the record of public culture is one from which women have been systematically excluded.

The religion of patriarchal culture validates this auxiliary status of women in various ways. Especially in the Genesis stories, women's creation is defined in such a way as to provide the aetiology of their secondary status. In the Bible this aetiology is given at two levels: the creation story and story of the fall. In the creation story, generic humanity is envisioned as male, the essential and original autonomous human person. Woman was created second as a derivative being. Her purpose is to be his helpmeet. Much apologia has gone into proving that no inferiority is implied by this description. The story, it is said, implies two equal persons who are complementary to each other.[8] This cannot be sustained. It focuses on the details and misses the shape of the forest. However much one may argue that "helpmeet" doesn't necessarily mean "inferior" or that the word for man and woman are different and coordinate words distinct from the word for generic humanity, Adam, this does not alter the basic *tendenz*, which has been consistently recognized and elaborated upon in the history of exegesis of the story from ancient rabbinical times.[9] The story of the creation of a woman from the rib of the original man to be his helpmeet clearly located "woman's place" as derivative and auxiliary. Its ideological character must be recognized in its fundamental reversal of actual biological experience, in which men are born from women, not women from men. To make Eve a creation from Adam is to make Eve in some sense Adam's daughter, a creature fashioned out of his body to serve him, not an autonomous person in her own right. Even an exegesis that regards the original Adam as androgynous, and sees Eve as the separation out of Adam of his "feminine side," only furthers this derivative and dependent status. The male alone is an autonomous whole person containing the full human essence. Woman is derived from him as a projection of a lower half or "feminine, bodily" side of himself to serve the bodily side of an automous personhood defined in male terms.[10]

The story of the fall actually continues this justification of women's place as a subordinate being by making it a consequence of sin. However much women may now chuckle over the fact that Adam appears as something of a passive personality, in the fall the mythology that made man first in creation but woman first in sin was not intended to praise woman's wit. The pangs of women and their domination by their husbands are then defined as the punishment laid upon Eve for her primary role in the fall. This is not intended to describe patriarchal domination as unjust. On the contrary, it is intended to describe it as a just punishment that defines her condition within history. To revolt against this status is to revolt against God.

Within the New Testament there is just the beginning of a hint that the eschatological liberation won by Christ in some sense overcomes this punishment of Eve and liberates women to a new equality. There is some evidence that a new equality *was* extended to women in the Church, represented by the synoptic Gospels and Acts and even in St. Paul. Whatever ambivalence is represented by Paul's dictum that women should cover their heads when they preach and prophesy because they seduced the angels (a story derived from Genesis 6, and elaborated in the Apographa) Paul does assume that women do participate in the catechetical and even the teaching community of the Church, contrary to synagogue custom.[11] The famous passage of I Corinthians 14, 34, that women should keep silent is almost certainly not from Paul, but derives from the second generation of the pastoral epistles from which it has been interpolated into the epistle of Paul.[12] Even in the Church Fathers, redemption in Christ is said to liberate the woman from the curse of Eve. But this is interpreted to mean that the Christian virgin no longer bears children in sorrow nor is she under the domination of her husband because she has neither husband nor children.[13] Neither Paul nor the Church Fathers are ready to contemplate an understanding of redemption that would liberate women from patriarchal oppression within marriage or sexual relations.

If women today are able to find any continuity with the biblical and Judaeo-Christian traditions at all (and many women feel that this is impossible) it cannot be by creating pseudo-apologia for these traditions. We must push the tradition beyond its own limits. Recognizing both men and women as autonomous equal persons "by nature," we must recognize the stories of the creation and the fall as themselves a part of the fall, as themselves expressions of male ideology justifying false power. We can pick up on the hint that speaks of male domination as the consequence of the fall; but we will be interpreting it in a way that it was not interpreted before, in judging patriarchy as sinful power rather than justified punishment. We also have the hint in the New Testament that redemption in Christ overthrows patriarchy and restores men and women to equality,[14] but we must recognize that the Church either quickly suppressed this idea or allowed it to be read only into the special status of the Christian virgin. It was never allowed to penetrate and judge the condition of women within the family structure itself. Even the Christian virgin was hardly promoted to public leadership, rather virginity itself became the source of a whole new fear and suppression of women. There are enough hints in the tradition that define the original and the eschatological condition of humanity as one of equality. We are undertaking a new development of this tradition when we try to encorporate this material into our present frame of reference in order to place patriarchy itself under judgment and to demand, in the name of redemption, a society liberated from male supremacy.

These structures of patriarchy define then the foundations of sexism in Western society. It has been validated by our religious teachings in a tradition that extends from the second millenium before the Christian era to the first systematic attacks—still uncompleted—on these assumptions in our own times. However, two further strata of male culture should be delineated in order to understand the full picture of the sexist psychology we have inherited. These two strata I will define as "misogyny" and "spiritual femininity." The misogynist tradition goes beyond the definition of women in terms of property, dependency and service. It defines women as the source of evil and, in some sense, inherently evil. This of course is suggested in the stories that make Eve not only secondary in creation but the source of sin in the world, either through the fall from Paradise or by the seduction of the angels through which the demonic beings were born. These stories tend to get elaborated in a misogynous manner in the later Jewish Apocrypha.

Another important source of misogynous images comes from the ceremonies of ritual purification that attempt to separate the sacred sphere from the unclean. Although contact with certain bodily fluids and unclean substances render the male unclean, women are in a sense inherently "unclean." Menstrual taboos define women as untouchables during half of their adult lives. The priest must be clean of all contact with women in order to approach the sanctuary. Women are forbidden access to the inner sanctuary and are excluded from the outer court during menstruation. Mother's blood becomes, as it were, a kind of demonic substance from which the male sacerdotal magic must carefully segregate itself. The exclusion of women from priesthoods and even liturgical participation in classical Christianity still depends on the covert remnants of this view of women as polluted beings who contaminate the male precincts of sacral power.[16]

Greek culture developed the experience of body alienation and suppression in more philosophical terms. It regarded the true self as the soul or consciousness and saw the body as a demonic alien that must be suppressed in order to develop the integrity of the true self. This dualism of body and soul was read out into the dualism of male and female to symbolize women as the expression of the demonic agency of the sexual and the carnal that attacks and subverts the regnant mind or reason. Men identify themselves with the mind, women with dangerous carnality. This identification of women with the lower half of body-soul dualism is especially developed in Aristotle, who divided humanity along the lines of this dualism into the "head people" and the "body people"; the dominators and the dominated. Males are by nature the "head people" who dominate; women are the "body people" who are by nature to be dominated. Aristotle would also extend this dualism along the lines of class and race, defining slaves and non-Greeks as servile persons. The free Greek male was the natural aristocracy of humankind. But male and female is the archtypal expression of this division of mankind into head and body people hierarchically defined as a relation of domination and subordination.[17]

This tradition was inherited by the Church Fathers who typically defined men and women along the lines of mind and body. But because they also saw the body as an evil and demonic principle and defined salvation as the suppression of bodily feelings, women came to be seen as special incarnations of evil or "carnality." The flight from the body and the world became specifically the flight from woman. However, women were also allowed to participate in this flight from carnality and the world. By suppressing their maternal and sexual being they too might become virgins and participate in the redeemed existence won by Christ. But because they were also defined more intrinsically as symbols of the carnal sphere to be repudiated, the female virgin had to undertake a far more total supression and repudiation not only of her bodily, but, in some sense, of her nature as well. Male virginity was defined as restoring the male to his "natural, spiritual virility," while the female virgin was described as "unnatural," having transcended her natural female nature and having become "unnaturally virile."[18] To a large extent, these asymetrical definitions of male and female attainments in the spiritual realm still define our culture, defining male cultural achievements as enhancing his masculinity, while defining female intellectual achievements as rendering her unfeminine.

Asceticism also defined the soul as feminine in relation to God or Christ. The flight of the soul from the body to the spiritual realm was symbolized as a bridal communion between the virgin soul and Christ. Thus the soul, while it is regarded as a masculine principle in relation to the body or in relation to dominated races, classes, women and physical nature, is regarded as spiritually feminine in relation to God. The relation is still one of hierarchical patriarchalism, but now it is mankind and the soul that are feminine in relation to the hierarchcal power and domination of God.

It was out of this dual level of male-female symbolism that there developed the split image of the feminine in Christianity—the split between spiritual femininity, symbolized by the Virgin Mary and Christian virgins and carnal femaleness, which is seen as the incarnation of the diabolic power of sensuality. This split continued to grow more and more intense during the Middle Ages until it erupted in a veritable orgy of paranoia in the late medieval period. It can hardly be a coincidence that the same period that saw Mariology reach the greatest heights of theological definition and refinement with the triumph of the doctrine of the Immaculate Conception in nominalist theology also saw the outbreak of witch hunts that took the lives of upwards of one million women between the 14th and the 17th centuries.

Modern discussions of the witch craze have tended to pass over this preponderance of women in the witch hunts as accidental or due to some peripheral demographic changes. The medieval inquisitors and theoreticians of witchcraft were much more explicit in their attribution of demonic tendencies specifically to the female nature. Their sensuality, their secondary and fallen existence, their lack of true rationality, which defined woman in the scholastic terminology borrowed from Aristotle as a "misbegotten male," even the maleness of Jesus that redeems men more than women, all these and many more stereotypes of evil femaleness are ransacked by the official theoreticians of witchcraft to define women and the devil as going naturally together.[19]

The other side of this identification of bodily femaleness with the demonic and subversive powers ever plotting against the higher life of men is the exaltation of the Virgin Mary as the feminine nature of the soul untouched by sexuality. Generally speaking this tradition of spiritual femininity did little to uplift the image of women in medieval Christianity because all real women "in the flesh" tended to be identified with the carnal Eve. In the courtly love tradition there begins a secularization of Mariology, but here too spiritual love is only possible outside of marriage and procreation. It was only with the Romantic backlash against the French Revolution that there developed a more general extension of the mariological tradition of spiritual femininity into a secular cultural image of women.

A more detailed view of the relationship between the Romantic view of women and secular industrial society will be developed in another piece in this collection, so I will not attempt to discuss this theme in detail.[20] It will be enough to summarize the two most critical elements in the new alignment of the traditional stereotypes of male and female nature. Changes in the role of religion played an important part in this shift. Traditional Catholicism had regarded virginity or consecrated widowhood as the highest expressions of the redeemed life and had given marriage a third-rate status. Seen as barely redeemed by its good end in procreation from the foul abyss of flesh and sexuality, ascetic spirituality could hardly develop a positive view of marriage as an arena of Christian virtue. Protestantism altered this view, negating the separate virgin life and reaffirming traditional patriarchal marriage. This had the effect of abolishing the one alternative life style other than marriage open to women provided by the religious order. Women were given no new role in the Church by

Protestantism because St. Paul's dictum that women should keep silent
was taken as normative. But the family was elevated as a center of moral
nurture. In Puritanism especially, the family became virtually an
ecclesiola or substructure of the church. The father became the pastor of
the family, with his wife and children as his congregation. Although Puritanism continued to stress the traditional patriarchal view that women
were created to bear children and to be the obedient and silent helpmeets
of their husbands, the balancing side of St. Paul's admonishment that husbands should love and cherish their wives was taken with new seriousness.
Some of the warm glow of the tradition of courtly love was imported into
marriage to soften the harsh language of patriarchal domination. Spiritual
compatibility and love came to be an important purpose and measure-
ment of marriage. Milton was the first to recognize that this new fusion of
marriage and love also demanded the escape hatch of divorce from incom-
patible marriages.[21]

This shift of the locus of moral nurture and spiritual community
from the religious community to the home took on a significance quite
unintended by the 16th century reformers. Between the 17th and 19th
centuries secularism eroded the established relationship of Church and
state and relocated religious life in the private sphere of personal life.
Instead of the traditional dualism between Church and world, with the
family located as part of the "world," secular bourgeois culture created a
dualism between the home and the world. The traditional spiritual virtues
became located in the home—the sphere of women. The Church too
gradually found itself located primarily in the private domestic sphere as
an extension of the home rather than in the public sphere as spiritual
mentor of kings. The new ideology of male and female "natures" that
became typical of post-revolutionary bourgeois society reflects this new di-
chotomy. At first this almost appears to be a reversal of the traditional
view of women as more sensual and less moral, spiritual and pious than
men. The 14th century witch hunters Henry Kramer and James
Sprenger, authors of the *Malleus Maleficarum*, could confidently locate
the etymology of the word "femina" as "lacking in faith." Women were
pictured as inherently subversive to constituted religious authority.

By the 19th century this view would have become incomprehensible.
Victorian society assumed that the bulwark of traditional religiosity was
women. Women were seen as inherently more spiritual and moral than
men, although this did not alter the traditional view of them as less rational. But as Beverly Harrison has pointed out, these virtues of morality,

spirituality and religiosity were located in women precisely at the point when they were losing ground in institutional expressions of public power.[22] The "real world" was now no longer the spiritual world that led up to the throne of God and descended downward to found the mighty ecclesiastic edifice that sanctioned public power. Theocracy had been dethroned. Now the "real world" was the material world, the world of science, technology and technical rationality. Men became "more materialistic" and women "more spiritual" at precisely the moment when the material world became the "real world" from which power flowed, and the spiritual world became an atavistic realm of private sentimentality that no longer interpenetrated the realm of power.

This new dualism between a private "feminized" religion and a secular world of power was fundamental to liberal Christianity. The ideologies of home and work, women and men, morality and rationality, virtue and power were decisively shaped along the lines of this new schizophrenia. The crisis created by the barbarism of modern technological society and the crisis of women in revolt against their domestication now have come together. They are two sides of the same crisis of a mariological femininity that locates the spiritual and humanistic values in the private, domestic sphere. The true significance of the women's movement as a challenge not only to traditional society but to modern secular society can only be understood if this relationship between the new feminine mystique and secularism is brought into the open and its various ramifications explored.

Yet the traditional view of women as more carnal and sexual than men did not disappear. The medieval division between spiritual femininity identified with the Virgin Mary and carnal femaleness identified with fallen Eve was now relocated along class and racial lines. Victorian society fused love and marriage, but love was still presumed to be spiritual and asexual. Proper married women were regarded as "above" sexual feeling. But this importing of the traditions of sexual repression into bourgeois marriage demanded its obverse side in the proliferation of houses of prostitution. Lower-class women bore the brunt of the double standard. The myths of the Virgin and the Whore divided into the middle-class world of repressed decorum and into the lower class world exploited for work and sexuality. The myth of the delicate woman who faints at the sight of a mouse is essentially a class myth that conceals its underpinnings in the world of sweatshops and brothels.

In the American South the same myth of the Virgin and the Whore could be organized along not only class but racial lines. The color symbolism of black women and white women as symbols of the bestial nature and the spiritual nature provided a kind of "color coding" for this division of women along class and racial lines into spheres of sexual repression and idealization and of brutalization and sexual exploitation. The Church itself was reshaped to sanction this new idealization of woman and the home, oblivious to the way this ideology was removing large sections of life— both the underworld of exploitation and the public world of power—from susceptibility to moral scrutiny and judgment. Religion as the original sanctioner of the inferiorization of women itself fell victim to its own trap. The woman and the clergyman find themselves ensconced in the same golden cage and bidden to sing sweet songs of gentleness, love, mercy and forgiveness that society reveres in its moments of private rectitude, but that it has no intention of allowing to interfere with the real business of running "the world."

Notes: Chapter I

1. For a discussion of women in Old Testament Law, see Phyllis Bird, "Images of Women in the Old Testament," in *Religion and Sexism: Images of Women in the Jewish and Christian Traditions*, Rosemary Radford Ruether, ed., New York: Simon and Schuster, 1974, ch. 2.

2. Simone, de Beauvoir, *The Second Sex*, New York: Bantam, 1961, pp. 84-7.

3. See Eleanor Flexner, *A Century of Struggle: The Woman's Rights Movement in the United States*, New York: Athanaeum, 1972.

4. Gunnar Myrdal, "A Parallel to the Negro Problem," *An American Dilemma*, New York: Harper, 1944, Appendix A, p. 1073.

5. J. B. Russell, *Witchcraft in the Middle Ages*, Cornell University Press, 1972, ch. 2.

6. Judith Hauptmann, "Images of Women in the Talmud," in *Religion and Sexism*, Rosemary Radford Ruether, ed., ch. 6.

7. Ruth Kelso, *Doctrine for the Lady of the Renaissance*, Illinois University Press, 1956.

8. See Phyllis Trible, "Depatriarchalizing in Biblical Interpretation," *J.A.A.R.*, XLI/I (March, 1973), 35-42; also George H. Tavard, *Women in Christian Tradition*, Notre Dame University Press, 1973, 4-11.

9. Theodor Reik, *The Creation of Woman*, New York: McGraw-Hill, 1973, pp. 39-67.

10. Rosemary Ruether, "Misogynism and Virginal Feminism in the Fathers of the Church," *Religion and Sexism*, Rosemary Radford Ruether, ed., ch. 5.

11. Bernard Prusak, "Women: Seductive Siren and Source of Sin?", in *Religion and Sexism*, Rosemary Radford Ruether, ed., ch. 3.

12. Robin Scroggs, "Paul: Chauvinist or Liberationist?", *The Christian Century* (March 15, 1973), pp. 307-9; *Ibid.*, "Paul and the Eschatological Woman," *J.A.A.R.* XL/3 (September, 1972), pp. 283-303.

13. See note 10 above.

14. Constance Parvey, "The Theology and Leadership of Women in the New Testament," in *Religion and Sexism*, Rosemary Radford Ruether, ed., ch. 4.

15. See note 11 above.

16. Clara Marie Henning, "Canon Law and the Battle of the Sexes," in *Religion and Sexism*, Rosemary Radford Ruether, ed., ch. 8.

17. Aristotle, *Politics*, I, 1-2.

18. See note 10 above.

19. *Malleus Maleficarum*, Pt. I, Q. VI. For a general discussion of the image of women in medieval thought see Eleanor Commo McLaughlin, "Equality of Souls, Inequality of Sexes; Woman in Medieval Theology," in *Religion and Sexism*, Rosemary Radford Ruether, ed., ch. 7. Also Michael Kaufman, "Spare Ribs: The Concept of Women in the Middle Ages and the Renaissance," *Soundings* (Summer 1973), vol. 66, no. 2, pp. 139ff.

20. "The Cult of True Womanhood and Industrial Society" (ch. 3).

21. William Haller, "Milton and the Law of Marriage," *Liberty and Refor-*

mation in the Puritan Revolution, New York: Columbia University Press, 1955, pp. 79-99; also William and Malleville Haller, "The Puritan Art of Love," *Huntington Library Quarterly* V, 235-71.

22. Beverley Harrison, "Some Ethical Issues in the Woman's Movement," unpublished paper presented to the American Society of Social Ethics, January 18, 1974; *Ibid.*, "Sexism and the Contemporary Church; When Evasion Becomes Complicity," in Alice Hageman, ed., *Women and Religion: Voices of Protest*, New York: Association Press, 1974.

Chapter II

Growing Up Male:
A Personal Experience

Eugene C. Bianchi

It has become increasingly clear in recent years that the churches and synagogues have contributed greatly to the long history of oppressing women. Yet in our renewed awareness of the plight of women we have failed to focus on a vast corollary problem. We have not seen quite so clearly that our religious institutions as upholders of cultural values have also fostered a perverted understanding of masculinity. Religious doctrines and practices, while seeming to place the male in positions of power, have in effect alienated men from vital dimensions of their own selfhood. To appreciate the ways by which males are shaped in a given spiritual and cultural matrix we need to make the serious reflective effort of gaining perspective on our "normal" formation as men. This means pulling back from the enveloping cultural atmosphere to gain distance for a critique of given social values concerning maleness.

Just as the issues surrounding current feminism impinge on what it means to grow up male in America these questions also relate most significantly to what it means to be authentically religious. I am suggesting at the start that Christianity, Judaism, or any other religion is profoundly vitiated by distorted modes of living either as a male or a female. The theological and churchly reforms since Vatican II, for example, will remain relatively superficial unless they are able to challenge the styles according to which we live our maleness and our womanliness. We will never develop our religious traditions in life-giving ways without grappling with the conscious and unconscious patterns that set our identities as men and women. Church reform in depth calls for radical rethinking and especially "re-feeling" our human formation as masculine and feminine.

I intend to approach this task through autobiographical reflection. How was I formed and deformed as a male whose forty-four years have been closely linked to the Christian Church in its Roman Catholic heritage? To explore my own story is much more than a search for concepts and examples that can be conveniently applied to the issue at hand. It is rather a journey to rediscover and reshape my own identity, self-meaning and self-worth. But such a project, which can be no more than initiated in this brief essay, is not simply one man's story. My autobiographical inquiry reflects in many ways the coming-to-be of other males in different traditions of the same culture. Although my experiences remain in some sense unique they mirror those of other men living in the same social milieu. It is up to the reader to decide where the patterns I describe fit his/her personal experiences of growing up and entering majority. The sensitive reader will know where to nuance and where to accommodate my tale.

Two other preliminary points are important. Autobiographical contemplation depends on creative memory and imagination. Although I want to be true to my past I will necessarily reshape that history according to my present outlook and feelings. I can never go home again. Yet it is precisely the genius and value of self-story telling that it reveals me to myself in the present as I stretch toward a more reconciled future. My history, far from being excess baggage, becomes a vehicle for self-realization in the present; scriptural writers as well as modern authors in literature and in psychology have repeatedly made that point. The second preamble note concerns my critical stand towards the Church in its pedagogy about maleness. If I were not able to say a number of positive things about Christianity I would have lost interest in it long ago as a vital source of life empowerment for me. I choose to emphasize the negative in this essay because it is deserved in light of Christian history and also because a wider educational and self-growth reason prompts such a hard reckoning. If we cannot challenge the previous we will never be open to and surprised by the new. If I cannot question critically how I was "marinated" as a male I will never experience what kind of man I may yet be.

I grew up in a patriarchal household where decision and power at nearly every turn resided in my father. I hasten to add that there were many occasions of mother getting her way, but it was done through behind-the-scenes cunning. Direct communication between equals was never a possibility for my parents. Obedience and submission expressed the given mode of interpreting the marriage injunctions to be obedient to husband and to God. The overt and subliminal message to the little boy was clear: women are subordinate, weak, ancillary. They are loving and affectionate, if a bit neurotic, but destined by nature for service and support roles towards men. This model of the feminine was continually reinforced by my mother's women friends, most of whom were church-influenced in corroborating their womanly self-image. Though my mother was born in the U.S.A. her upbringing was in an immigrant Italian home where the traditional roles for women, housewife and child-rearing were almost exclusively stressed. Women might work for wages outside the home in a laundry or a cannery, but this was seen as a part-time financial expediency, never as the vocation or proper place for the wife. The socially and religiously induced fear of abandoning children and household duties carried dire consequences in my mother's perspective. I am both immensely grateful for her loving care and conscious of the limitations of that expression of woman's role. It subconsciously taught me what to expect from other women in my life.

Although my father had explicitly rejected his Italian church background as far as belief and practice were concerned, he was still very much the inheritor of an exceedingly male-chauvinist culture. For centuries Italy has inextricably mixed the religious and the secular. In Italian *pappa* means both father of a family and pope. My father's man/woman role models were derived from the division of labor that obtained in the tenant farmer experiences of the Tuscan countryside. I have traveled back in imagination to the hilly farm where my father was born, especially since my visit there in the early 1960s. In that frugal and arduous existence I visualize the grandmother I never knew going through the routine interactions of her day. What did my father learn there that fashioned his attitude towards women? My grandmother was a fragile woman bound down by the incessant demands of a large family and by the chores of a rude agricultural life. It is said that as a very young woman she taught school. I wonder if she later mused in disappointment at the hard and fixed patterns that her married role demanded. Was she able to communicate beyond the level of survival needs with the husband who left at dawn for the fields and returned tired for food and sleep in the evening?

It is risky to read my father's reactions to women into his father—

allowance must be made for difference of temperament and personality. But if I can judge from my own responses toward my wife, sometimes unconscious or at least unexpressed, I know something of the power of repeating parental patterns. I have been surprised at how deeply engraved in my psyche are certain behaviors toward my wife that imitate my father. I catch myself parenting and domineering her in ways that reproduce paternal memories. If after all my formal education and reflection on these matters I find myself coming on with the negative patterns of my father, it seems likely that his male behavior was formed in those early interactions observed in a peasant household. Despite the obnoxious aspects of Latin *machismo*, however, the Italian male has generally preserved certain traits of warmth and tenderness that I find lacking in Anglo-Saxon and other northern forms of male dominance. For the Latin male emotions are more easily shown, and a kind of earthy humanism allows him to cross the line occasionally into "woman's work."

Another side of my father-model concerned the struggle to succeed in American society. I had learned early that woman's place was in the home as a rearer of children and man's destiny was a worldly life of striving and attainment. But for the son of an immigrant father the American success dream was ambiguous and anxiety-producing. The national version of the Puritan work ethic held out its incentives, rewards and demands. Yet the son knew that the cards to "making it," to showing the proper signs of holy election and thus of self-worth and self-acceptance, were stacked against the immigrant working man. No doubt these hard requirements for achieving personhood in America were in good measure a cause of my father's frustrations. The land of opportunity also inculcated an intense spirit of competition among males. The majority of men at every level of our society suffer feelings of inadequacy and self-hatred in the face of the dogged competition that makes the impossible demand that they all be winners.

The external performance rules for becoming a valuable male person in a competitive, possession-amassing culture created special strains on me. I had no family models of American success, that is, secularized salvation. Could I be saved, would I be accepted and thus redeemed by the real Americans who watched and judged my performance? I was compelled to push my modest athletic talent to the utmost to win, to be recognized. Would I make the grades in school that might launch me toward achievement and consequent self-worth as a male? I sometimes wonder how much the anxiety and insecurity of growing up in this way contributed to my decision to enter the relative security of the Jesuit Order. Personal efforts and psychological counseling in recent years have helped me become aware of and criticize past performance conditioning. I have begun to ignore the previously ubiquitous gaze of my cultural watchers, and I am risking decisions and self-evaluations arising from the dictates of my own organism.

The parochial Church and school taught me lessons, hidden and manifest, about the relationships between men and women. The division of roles in the parish was obvious. Priests, all men of course, were of the highest importance and influence; they made the major decisions about parish policy. Even more significantly they alone performed the saving functions of the sacraments. A ladies' altar society served the sanctuary and did other kitchen and cleaning jobs at parish functions. As youngsters we automatically associated the priests with the realm of mind, spirituality and public power. Women in the parish were examples to us of bodily concerns, lesser devotional piety and private, service roles. As a young boy I could not have articulated the message that was taking shape in images and indirect symbols concerning women. In retrospect the Church was preaching in a variety of ways its dual attitude towards women. The ruling male ecclesiastics both feared and deprecated women. Afraid of the ancient and mysterious power of the feminine, they treated her as a perpetual minor fated to be under the control of men and their institutions.

Perhaps nowhere did this become clearer for boys than in their special prerogative to serve at the altar. Only males could actually approach the holy books and sacred vessels. Anatomy was indeed destiny, although the parishioners of Sacred Heart Church in Oakland, California, would have been shocked to learn that their parish was orchestrating Freudianism in every facet of its life. We did not reflect then that the exclusion of girls from altar service because of their nature and not their talent must have been a depressing experience for the more sensitive ones. Nor did we realize that the images of women as inferior, unclean and dangerous were already beginning to form as we answered *Et cum spiritu tuo* and walked with solemn decorum about the sanctuary. Though we did not consciously formulate the thought, we were responding to a purer male spirit, male priest, male God. The male projection of woman as unclean and a source of perilous temptation was verbally stated in certain liturgical passages and repeatedly stressed in moral preachments on sex.

But the nonverbal presentation of the same themes was to be witnessed in both the exclusion of women from the sanctuary and in the construction of the confessional. The wall of separation, the screen and the darkness, were designed not only for privacy but also to protect the priest from solicitation and seduction. The words of Canon Law about these matters confirm the attitude expressed in the design of the confessional.

Yet the American Catholic Church of the 1930s and 1940s had its version of superior women in the nuns and especially in the Virgin Mary and a few saints. We looked on the nuns as a special, mysterious and separate group. Yet the role of disciplinarian that was forced upon them in overly large classes of unruly grammar school pupils continued in the male psyche the authoritarian, nagging image of his earliest female overseers. The nuns were viewed as an other-worldly, sequestered group who were out of contact with the mainstream of social life. Little was known of their personal lives in the convent building (where I waxed many a floor). I recall my dismay and soul-threatening horror at the news that my second-grade nun had left the congregation; she had "run off" to marry! My scandalized mind reeled at the thought of such a preternatural creature descending into carnality and ordinariness.

The nuns appeared to live a confined and rote-like existence. We saw them moving silently in black-robed groups during dawn hours to Mass or herding children to confession on Fridays. As a category they were perceived as holy, that is removed from the typically human. But their life of controlled milieu, or of operating in supervised teams, contrasted sharply with the independent activities of priests. I was actually observing an accentuated form of the general societal practice of controlling women under the supposedly noble guise of protecting them. Occasionally a nun's personality would shine through in spite of the homogeneous community life; yet nuns came across as mere parish fixtures. They were part of the Catholic parish plant as familiar and expected as the sanctuary lamp, the confessional or First Friday Masses.

This comparison to things and events is intentional. For they were Church property to be disposed of solely according to the directives of male ecclesiastical law. Even when nuns had more education or natural ability than the parish priest, he alone made the important decisions. The nuns were ancillary creatures who faithfully repeated to us what the hierarchy instructed them to say. This habit of submission to authority in matters of public and private religion and morality was instilled into us by the conduct and teaching of the nuns. Before Vatican II this attitude was so deeply inculcated that even Catholic college students found it hard to avoid guilt and anxiety when they took critical positions against the Church's stand. It took me many years to make truly independent judgments on issues of religion and morality.

As they served to form the image of woman in the consciousness of this growing lad, the nuns could not have escaped Thomas Aquinas' cruel appellation of "misbegotten males." It is important to note that whatever improved status the nuns enjoyed was accorded them in the degree to which they denied their womanness. They had given up sexual relations and had covered their womanly beauty with starched coifs, breastpieces and heavy woolen habits. Yet, as Rosemary Ruether points out (Chapter I), even this sacrifice of virgin dedication did not bring them equality with men in Church life. Although the Catholic woman of my boyhood certainly had her religious pecularities, it is not difficult to find anaolgies with Protestant and Jewish women.

The Reformation had taken women out of cloistered convents only to put them back into restricted parochial roles as subservient wives and congregational auxiliaries for church suppers. A number of Protestant churches in recent years have opened their seminaries to women; these female seminarians are challenging the theory and practice of their male-dominated ecclesial institutions. In an ecumenical era, these women provide encouraging examples of yet unrealized possibilities for Catholic women to enter any level of Church life. It should be added however that the mere substitution of women for men in the clergy will not renew the ministry. Our understanding of ministry itself needs to shift from hierarchical castes towards fellowships for the sharing of personal gifts.

In Judaism, the maleness of the rabbinate and the separation of men and women in traditional synagogues, with men taking leading positions in liturgy and the anti-feminine meaning of certain prayers and rites—all testify to the derivative place of women. Although this situation is starting to change in Reform congregations, it is frequently defended with unconvincing arguments by Jewish spokesmen. They point to woman's exalted place in the Jewish home, where sacredness is to be sought in religious observances and in familial duties. Yet the explanation sounds like a Jewish version of the glorification of housewifery to maintain a status quo in which men continue to exercise dominance. Moreover, the more traditional position about the demands of "modesty" in excluding women from

leading synagogue functions smacks both of negative male sex projections
and of the depreciating aspects of the ancient taboo of uncleanness that
was fixed on the female.

In addition to Catholic lay women and nuns, devotion to Mary significantly influenced my attitude and approach towards women. Mary
held a special place in my religious life for twenty-five years. I remember
many processions to honor her—novenas to Our Lady of this or that, the
fifteen mysteries of the rosary that became such a hallmark of Catholic
piety and the special Marian Masses that dotted the liturgical calendar.
Mary was to us a person of incomparable suasion with God. But even her
power was derived from a male savior figure. She was at best a sacred go-
between, a motherly broker of grace from the God/Father. She mirrored
in a heavenly mode the soft and indirect styles by which our earthly
mothers often got what they wanted from authoritarian fathers. *Ad Jesum*
(read *Deum*) *per Mariam* was the capsule phrase for this phenomenon. I
have come to wonder how much this devotional stress on Mary was in
fact a substitute for pacifying our mothers for the daily frustrations and
self-denying burdens they were forced to bear in a society that so firmly
limited their human potential. Prayerful contact with Mary helped these
women to believe that "offering it all up" would bring blessings on their
families. It helped them to embrace their constricted lot in this life in hope
of enjoying a Mary-like exaltation in the next world.

We failed to see how much Mary was an ethereal, asexual projection
of a Church dominated by a massive male consciousness. Ruether traces
this spiritualizing of the mother of God and relates it brilliantly to the
privatized world of womanly religion in the 19th century (Essay II).
Marian devotion was teaching me to distance women both in my earlier
years and in the seminary. The great emphasis on her purity in my gram-
mar- and high-school days had the twofold effect of making me fearful
and anxious about my own expanding sexuality and of making me neuro-
tically concerned about the danger of serious sin in friendships with girls.
It took a long time to work my way out of these inhibitions, and I could not
have done it without the assistance of sensitive women.

Even now there must be in me an unconscious residue of that long
training in sexual alienation based on exhortations to emulate the purity
of Mary. In another way she was the glorified embodiment of a de-sexed
mother image, a symbol for men to use in cherishing their mothers without
dealing with them as enfleshed women. It was also a figurative way of not

having to relate to other women as equal, though different, humans. The etherializing of the Virgin furthermore allowed us a path for escaping from the affirmation of feminine qualities in our male selves. We denied what Jung referred to as our *anima* in a civilization that held out success to tough maleness. By this mode of strange indirection Marian devotion was unwittingly preparing us for the destructive violence of much male life, a theme that I will explore later.

The eternal-feminine pedestal resulted in still another deprecation of woman in our male thought processes and behaviors. The Church that enshrined a version of woman as spiritual and pure also warned against the other extreme of the feminine, Eve the temptress, the whore who threatens male rationality and dominance. Primitive fears of woman as mysterious and dangerously powerful continued in the medieval destruction of witches. This scapegoating of women persists in more subtle ways in the various forms of social discrimination and in the ecclesiastical culture of Catholicism. For centuries Church offices have been controlled by men trained according to the celibate norms of monasticism. Because the celibate must make special ascetic efforts to preserve his eccentric life pattern he tends to see woman as a threat to his virtue. With this heritage the Catholic Church has been more prone than other religious bodies to visualize woman at either extreme, Mary or Eve, Mother of the Year with eight church-going children, or uncontrolled and preying female. For this reason woman was either to be adored or ignored, glorified or avoided, but never treated as an equal and full person. For us no middle ground existed for honest interaction.

Moreover, placing woman in heaven (Mary) or hell (Eve) became a convenient way of removing her from earth where she could compete with men for a just share of material and human resources. In his latest document on the Blessed Virgin and modern women Pope Paul VI displays the ambiguities of one who is heir to this polar vision of woman. His attempt to interpret the symbolism of Mary as a model for self-affirming and creative modern woman is admirable; but the strictures of his own Church continue to belie the new interpretation. Women are excluded from decision-making positions in the Church and their free choice in matters of birth control and abortion is severely restricted.

It would, however, be both too easy and also incorrect for those of other persuasions to dismiss these aspects of Marian tradition that I inherited as only a Roman aberration. Similar patterns of male/female relationships characterize not only other churches but also our culture at large. I have labeled this well-entrenched masculine mentality as psychic celibacy (cf.pp. 87ff.). Although distinct from physical celibacy as practiced in Catholicism, psychic celibacy is a more pervasive and imposing phenomenon. It consists in keeping woman mentally and emotionally at arm's length. It is in fact the core dogma of our patriarchal era. Woman can be exalted as wife, virgin, mother or deprecated (and enjoyed) as temptress, playmate, whore. In whatever way this male projection works, woman is object, non-equal, manipulated, distanced. With myths and rituals different from those of Catholic Marianism, therefore, our society embraces a key feature of that devotion.

For the most part, my life has been located in male places. An all-male Catholic high school preceded entry into an all-male Jesuit Order. I lived in male lodges or clubs that reinforced the polar views and feelings about women I have described. Woman was pure virgin or perilous temptation to rational control. She could also, in male-supervised situations, be a helpful servant and a source of comfort. But in my male milieu she was more menace than promise. I recall the repressive sexual morality that we were taught in high school and in the early years of our religious training. Sex, that powerful and attractive force in us, was desired but feared because it threatened decision-making control and order in patriarchy; the rational mind, the higher spirituality might be placed in jeopardy. Until the last few years I have not begun to listen seriously to the experience of women; living with one who struggles to free herself from the layers of oppression has constituted my chief learning experience. The sexual guilts we felt about threatening the system that formed us were projected onto woman as the amoral enticer who could steal away our prerogatives. We had to guard against the misfortune of Samson who ended badly by trading power for sex.

I was struck recently by the importance of this experiential lesson when I was talking about women's liberation with a Jesuit friend. This enlightened and open-minded person agreed in theory about women's deprived status and the need to ameliorate it. But he showed an emotional revulsion at the mention of a woman scholar who boldly proclaimed this situation in face-to-face encounters with theologians. It is one thing to think about inequities and quite another to confront an outspoken woman who challenges our masculine, emotional expectations.

I believe that the importance of maintaining public power for rea-

sons of personal self-esteem is at the root of Catholic and Episcopalian opposition to the ordination of women. This is also the basis for refusal to
admit a married priesthood in Catholicism. If the priesthood is opened to
women and married men, the old temple of monasticism, with its privileges and perquisites, might again collapse on Samson. To preserve
power and status with their distorted promises of self-worth, the mutually
alienating, male/female dualisms are maintained. Exclusion from priesthood takes place automatically for men who have associated themselves
with women by a kind of contagion. For they have been infected, according to the diagnosis of the clerical mind, by intimacy with the opposite
pole of the male/female dualism.

   St. Ignatius Loyola, the Jesuit founder, unwittingly testified to this
dichotomizing male projection when in his Rules for the Discernment of
Spirit (cf. Rule 12 in *The Spiritual Exercises*) he compared woman's conduct to Satan's. The devil acts like a woman, he asserts, in that she
becomes ferocious and conquering when a man ceases to exercise domination over her. Yet St. Ignatius had female friends and helpers in his growing institution. These however were always women of nobility who had
transcended typical femaleness to approximate the status of men, that is
they possessed inherited wealth and they exercised public power. This
need to foster the dualisms that make woman into an almost other or
pseudo-species is also at the core of the strictures against homosexuality
both in my own religious training and in our society at large. Certain
traits and desires are termed effeminate. That is, these dimensions are
viewed as imperiling that one-sided combination of masculine qualities
that are deemed necessary for the maintenance of patriarchal hegemony in
society.

   Seminary education continued to strengthen the cultural dualisms
that uphold masculinity and subordinate the feminine. Throughout these
years of my schooling the real history of women was either unknown, ignored or subsumed under a male perspective. If we examine the history of
the relatively few canonized women saints in Catholicism we discover that
most of them are classified as virgins. The sex-denying aspects of becoming
an ecclesiastical virgin are in themselves a rejection of the feminine and a
strange sort of approximation to male status. Beyond this limitation few
women have been designated as Doctors of the Church. Although it is true
that most women were deprived of formal education until recent times,
many holy women in ages past were educated in religious matters. Yet

men constructed criteria for judging feminine sanctity in a way that kept women out of the realm of the rational or intellectual implied in the title Doctor of the Church.

The alienating dichotomies between male and female, with their consequences for superior/inferior inferences, followed each phase of seminary education. We heard nothing of the anthropological discussion about the highly significant place held by women in the early history of our species. We were not made aware that not only agriculture but cultural communication probably developed in ancient tribal settlements from the closer interaction of women. A number of myths, such as that of the Ibibio tribe in Africa, relate to a cult of the great mother, the symbol of feminine power and wisdom. The myths tell us that men stole the fearsome power of woman. In our study of the humanities and ancient classics we learned that the field of idea and of history belonged to man, the maker. In the Hellenistic and later Renaissance worlds woman was associated with nature and body, zones to be controlled by rational man. In theology our appropriation of the Judeo-Christian tradition was accompanied by a denial of the finite feminine matrix of our earthliness. Had not the transcendent Father, Yahweh, put down the false mother gods of fertile Canaan? Later various forms of Christian Platonism would subdue the tribal goddesses of the barbarians. The Hebrew prophetic tradition would eventually evolve into a kind of apocalypticism that also deprecates earth mother in its search for a purer other-worldly messianic existence.

When I look back at my life I realize more acutely that what we learn as true doctrine is often an ideology constructed to bolster well-established practices of individuals and institutions. Theology, as it relates to man-woman relations, often portrays this use of doctrine as ideology. When I went from teaching in an all-male high school to years of studying theology I was unconsciously using Church tenets to prop up a mode of acting and thinking that was already male-dominant. In that San Francisco high school we knew that boys as subjects for education were more important than girls. It was unquestioned that the future leaders of society would be men. In the study of theology our convictions were confirmed by teachings about a male God, male Christ and male virtues. It was taken for granted that a masculine hierarchy would rule over women, whether nuns or laywomen. These groups would be forever excluded from positions in the Church hierarchy. Theology as ideology corroborated and justified such thinking by assuring us that it was God's will, fixed in the laws of nature, that females should serve males.

Moreover, the Bible was filled with examples that could be used to show how firmly God had mandated male superiority. These divinely sanctioned patterns were so constraining that in moral theology we could wink at a sexual double standard that allowed men freedoms that were denied to women. Theological theory taught us to believe with greater security that what we had been doing all along was right. Theology became a source for upholding the stereotypes we had actually put into practice or at least believed, such as: women are hyperemotional and consequently can't be trusted with responsibility; women are non-intellectual and best suited for homemaking and child-rearing, as well as service and esthetic pursuits. Our theological ideology in brief was denying feminine creativity; it was suppressing the individual personhood and potential of women. As with all stereotypes our theological perspective forced women into generic and subservient categories.

An added reason for not coming to grips with this antifeminist direction in theology and Church structure was the acquiescent attitude of women themselves. Church-related women so thoroughly internalized their oppression that they embraced it as a divine calling. We were immersed in the accepted scheme of things without understanding that our theories and policies often contradicted core elements of Christian faith. I do not mean by this to excuse our complicity; we should have known better. But I want to underscore the fact that Christians need to look first and especially at the patterns of sin, brokenness and oppression within our own camp before undertaking a critique of the wider society. Without such self-scrutiny we increase the zone of hypocrisy that stifles religious credibility for so many in our time. Moreover, we can be reminded of another corollary fact that should contribute to enlarging an ecumenical and humble spirit among us. The churches were not originators of the contemporary feminist movement. Others led the way and only after considerable exposure to the movement did church people appreciate its congruence with the implications of their own faith.

Yet I am convinced that man/woman relations, as evidenced in theory and in practice in the Church, continue to negate essential dimensions of Christian faith in at least two ways. First these oppressive concepts and structures contradict the crucial Gospel emphasis about being equal persons in Christ. Paul summarizes this theme very well in a few places, although he was a partial victim of the chauvinism of his own age. In Galatians he tells us: "There is neither Jew nor Greek, there is neither slave nor free, there is neither male nor female; for you are all one in Christ Jesus" (Gal. 3:28). This ideal of an equal community of brothers and sisters was maintained more in the breach than in the observance through the centuries in matters of ecumenism, race and man/woman relations. But the theme of equality and oneness remains a central perspective against which we and our institutions are judged. Some have tried to mitigate the New Testament ideal as realized by the Church by affirming equality in Christ, but with different roles for men and women. While variety and diversity are necessary and healthy, the concept of difference of roles has frequently been used to cloak injustices. When the differences of role are shaped in such a way as to discriminate against a class of persons they cannot be whitewashed to pass for Gospel values. In Ephesians, Paul sounds a similar chord when he asserts that Christ is our peace because he has broken down the "dividing wall of hostility" to reconcile those who were alienated from one another (Eph. 2:14). Yet we deny this unifying, reconciling force in our lives when we uphold structures in the Church supportive of male dominance and female subordination. In doing this we foster human estrangement and inhibit the mutuality of equals whose gifts can heal and complement one another. Put another way, we obstruct friendship that demands equality in dialogic interaction.

There is yet a second way more proper to men by which we say "no" to the essence of Christian faith through our mentality and forms of male chauvinism. Faith by its very nature calls for an attitude of trust, risk, acceptance and dependence on a benevolent divine Spirit greater than ourselves. Male chauvinism on the contrary implies an intense kind of works-righteousness, a hopeless pursuit of proving to ourselves and to others our acceptableness and worth based on performing and achieving. The dichotomies projected by the male between mind and body, power and submissiveness, leader and led place man in the active, superior and attaining role. It is an exaggeratedly Promethean style that rejects finitude, passivity, receptiveness and the listening sensitivity of woman or, rather, those very obscured, undeveloped "feminine" qualities within each man. We are what we make, not what we feel, experience and receive. We attain value as persons, we are saved by our own strivings; we build the male Tower of Babel, our phallic symbol, to thrust our way into heaven. In myriad ways our culture has taught us that if we would be valuable persons we must be forever proving ourselves to others. We are unable to desist from the self-defeating pursuit of righteousness and simply accept the blessing of God as a gentle breeze against our faces. In this mad quest for a secularized justification and salvation we deny the heart of the act of faith that calls upon us as men to activate the receptive and accepting dimensions of our being.

My pilgrimage to move away from the chauvinist attitudes I learned in my family, Church and society has consisted in a gradual education of awareness and action during the last six years. I certainly have not "arrived" in overcoming all stereotypes and prejudices in male/female relations. But some headway has been made. I attribute this progress more to concrete happenings than to conceptualizing the issue, although I have also been much influenced by the literature of the feminist movement. Yet the deepest formation of sensibilities for me has resulted from living with a woman who has been developing her own feminist self-understanding. Some way-stations on our journey are clear in memory; others perhaps as important are lost in the sweep of life. The last essay in this volume expands at greater length on our mutual efforts to extricate ourselves from years of sexist conditioning. Here I would like to touch only in the briefest way on some of the milestones along the road.

I remember the early years of our marriage and my wife's need to establish a public involvement outside the house. Articles and books on aspects of feminism came into our home, and I was experiencing the growth of her own sense of self-confidence as a woman of talent and potential. There were exchanges, sometimes calm and complementary, sometimes emotional and angry, about expectations and roles and attitudes in our married life. Women friends became increasingly important to her and, later, friendships with men. As our understanding about, and actions in, the relationship changed, the marriage contract needed occasional renewal and adjustment. We divided household chores in a fair way, although this is ever-shifting territory. She legally engineered the return of her birth-given name, and I began to give a course on man/woman liberation and spiritual growth. This class has repeatedly been one of my best teaching experiences. We are both more aware of sexism in the media, in economic and political life, as well as in cultural patterns generally. Yet I do not claim to have overcome my sexism any more than I have washed away all my racism. I am in process however; I see things with new eyes.

None of these life events is monumental. Yet in the very ordinariness of my journey to this point is a deep challenge to religion, theology and myself. This challenge can be put as a simple question: Are we willing to begin again, to question the premises of our masculine indoctrination? The way we answer that question will determine to a great extent the rebirth and revitalization of our personal and institutional lives. Church, synagogue and believer must cease living the half-life of exaggerated maleness. If we listen to the feminine in ourselves (not that feminine that is only a feminized version of the male power/dominance syndrome), we can learn as men to be sensitive, open to repressed feelings and become sharing and empathetic. We will thus dispose ourselves to a more genuine experience of faith. This means receptiveness to the divine Spirit who can enlighten and transform us beyond anything we can achieve through our own efforts alone. Such a faith will prepare us for authentic social mission that requires a fully equal sense of co-humanity among men and women who would serve God's purposes in the world. To be able to begin again, to experience rebirth, calls for repeated change of heart, that quality called *metanoia* in Christian Scriptures and referred to as "the turning" in Jewish tradition. But this conversion or turning cannot take place in an atmosphere of repression and oppression among men and women. It calls not for male dominance but rather for an equal dialogic relationship between the masculine and the feminine within ourselves as men, with women as our peers, and within our religious and social intitutions.

Chapter III

The Cult of True Womanhood and Industrial Society

(From Machismo to Mutuality)

Rosemary Ruether

The home and the family is often assumed to be a primordial unit shaped by biological and psychological characteristics that pre-exist and are the foundation of all society. The outcry against any change in the role of women is always based on this assumption of the primordial and unchangeable characteristics of the family. Any changes in the family are treated as undermining society as a whole. But this notion of the unchanging family is very misleading because in actuality the nuclear family as we have come to know it is a product of changes that took place in Europe in the period from the late 15th to the 18th centuries. The family as it presently exists is an anomaly in social history and has a specific compensatory function in relationship to modern industrial society. It is only by understanding these changes that the type of socialization of women in the family in modern society becomes apparent. Only in this perspective can we begin to see the way in which the family functions as the unique realm of heterosexual intimacy, and woman becomes the high priestess of this realm of "intimacy" over against collective economic and political life.

In traditional societies marriage was not the union of two persons but an alliance of two families. It was a tribal alliance for economic and political purposes, and the choice of the two partners involved was secondary, if not irrelevant. Women particularly had little or no choice in whom they married. In medieval Christendom this was the basic approach to all marriages in the upper classes. In addition to this the Church maintained a negative view towards marriage as a realm of spiritual or moral values. In the Augustinian tradition the sexual act, even within procreative marriage, was inherently sinful, redeemed only by its good end in procreation. The act itself remained essentially debasing, and this debasing character of sex was passed on to the child as the taint of original sin. This view of sex effectively cut off the possibility of viewing sexual communion as real interpersonal communion in any spiritual sense. In the courtly love tradition love was possible only when divorced from sex and marriage. By the same token the family could not be viewed as a spiritual community analogous to the Church. The Jewish patriarchal view that saw the family as the basic unit of religious community, an idea that is also implied in the New Testament Pastoral Epistles, could not be developed in classical Christianity as long as this ascetic view of marriage prevailed. The truly committed Christian who wished to worship God fully could be only a celibate. Marriage was a third-rate option conceded to those weak members of the Church who were unable to rise to perfection. Its purpose was solely procreative, an unfortunate necessity that did not alter the vile character of the means to this end. Within such a view the ideal of "Christian family" as either a love relationship between spouses or as a community of values where its members were nourished in the faith could not really develop. The image of marriage remained under the negative sign of ascetic antisexuality throughout the Middle Ages.

Protestantism was to reject this ascetic view of the inferiority of marriage to virginity just as it rejected monasticism as the Christian way of perfection and restored the biblical patriarchal view of the family as a realm of religious nurture. In the process it also championed a new view of conjugality as a love relationship between spouses, although this was not allowed to challenge the traditional patriarchal view of the subordination of women. The marital relation for women was still defined as one of bearing children and being under the domination of their husbands. Yet, Protestantism borrowed some of the idealization of love from the courtly love tradition to soften and idealize the conjugal relationship. In the medieval tradition love could exist only as a sublimated, distant relationship with an unattainable woman who represented the spiritual womanhood of the Virgin Mary. Romantic love could only take place outside procreative marriage.

The Protestant—particularly the Puritan—tradition began the fusion of romantic love and conjugality. The family was thus enormously elevated in its ideological role in society. No longer a mere unfortunate biological necessity conceded by the Church despite its debasing nature, marriage now became the moral unit of society, a sub-unit of the Church as the community for the nourishment of moral and religious growth. The harsh patriarchal view of women was softened by the glow of romantic love. Catholicism was eventually to catch up with this Protestant development with its cult of the Holy Family and the childhood of Jesus.

As Philippe Aries has shown in his pioneering book, *Centuries of Childhood*, this new ideology of conjugality and the family corresponded to an evolutionary change in the character of the family itself that drastically altered its social role. Marriage among the bourgeois did not have the tribal character of the landed nobility for whom marriage continued to be a coalition of landed properties to consolidate the economic and political power of landholding families. For the nobility the only child who was important was the heir. The second son might be sent to the Church. The girls were bartered off in inter-tribal bargaining. Younger children mingled with bastard offspring and the children of servants. There was little sense of a distinct community of children and parents as a conjugal unit. Children were treated as members of the servant class. They were sent at an early age to act as valets, pages to wait at table and perform other servant functions for the adult society. This was their apprenticeship in adult society, which began at the age of seven or eight. At twelve or thirteen, an academically inclined youth of the more affluent classes was away at the university. There was little notion of siblings as a community to be reared in close relationship to their parents, nor of childhood as an extended period of dependency. Children from the first mingled with other children and adults who were not their parents and at an early age began to contribute to adult society.

As Aries has shown, the modern nuclear family is the result of an evolution that gradually did away with the complex extended family of earlier times. This type of family was pioneered by the bourgeois while the older types of family existed much longer among the nobility and the poor. It was only in the 19th century that the bourgeois family became the general norm for society as a whole. The heir was no longer distinguished so sharply from the younger children, but the younger children were set apart from servants and bastards who were eliminated from the home or at least placed in servants' quarters so they no longer grew up with the legitimate offspring. The home became privatized. Its earlier public character as a thoroughfare in which intimate functions such as childbirth and dressing were treated as public functions disappeared. Private bedrooms became clearly marked off from more public parts of the house. Servants and retainers no longer slept in the same rooms with the master. The social world was gradually thrust out of the home. The conjugal family as a community of parents and children withdrew into a new privacy that drew them together as a unit and distinguished them more and more from those who were not immediate members of this privileged unit. Childhood came to be seen as a separate era of life, clearly distinct from adulthood and entailing a longer period of formation. No longer were children little adults to be thrust into apprenticeship roles in adult society. Instead, childhood was seen as a time of extended innocence and plasticity to be molded by moral guardians. Parents—uniquely the mother—came to be seen as this molder of childhood innocence. Earlier, children were not so regarded. Born tainted with original sin they saw and participated in sex at an early age. Now, in the privatized family, childhood came to be seen as a pre-fallen state innocent of sexuality and to be kept innocent of it as long as possible. A magic circle of sexual innocence was drawn around womanhood and childhood, and the rough world of raw emotions was thrust outside. The home became an Eden of unfallen purity to be protected against the outside world. Mothering now became a full-time occupation and childhood nurturing a lifetime project that was expected to engage a woman's total moral and emotional energies. Rousseau's *Emile* summed up these views for an era. The family progressively lost its earlier social, political and economic functions. But it drew in the more on a newly extended definition of private intimacy and long-term childhood nurture, which now became its chief functions.

This privatization of the home meshed with the alienation of productive functions from the home in industrial development. The home, once an intrinsic unit of production where the basic tools and goods of daily life were made, began to lose these functions. At the same time male work that once took place in shops or fields in or around the home became increasingly socialized and alienated from it. Women at the same time began to lose their own productive work as well as the integration of their lives with male work. The home was refashioned from a producer to a consumer unit in society. It became concentrated exclusively on interpersonal intimacy and extended child nurture. With the loss of a servant class, who entered socialized work at the end of the 19th century, the middle-class wife also became the domestic servant who freed the male for the industrial work day. A new type of family and a new definition of woman's role as a caste came into being that had not existed in the West in so limited a form. Women, having lost the productive work of the home that was theirs in an earlier society, also lost much of the earlier mobility that allowed them to participate in social production. Poor women to be sure were being drawn into factory production under highly exploitative wages and conditions. But the woman entrepreneur still common in the 17th or 18th century began to become a rarity by the 19th century. The ideology of womanhood became concentrated exclusively on functions in the new bourgeois home.

In Victorian times this ideology of the home as the realm of rest and restoration for work, child nurture and interpersonal intimacy was still imbued with the psychology of sexual repression. The cult of romantic love still demanded that true love be nonsexual. Intimacy and emotionality could be good only if it was "pure"—sublimated and separated from the physical. Children were supposed to be "innocent" until adulthood. But for women this childhood innocence became their permanent identity. Girls were supposed to know nothing of sex until marriage and even then were supposed to remain as detached from their unfortunate biological roles as possible. Only by remaining the lifelong sexual innocent could woman be transformed into that "mother" who in turn was to nurture a new generation of innocents. Women and children were set apart in the unfallen Eden of asexual purity. The bourgeois wife and mother partook of all the aura of the Virgin Mary and the lady of courtly love. In her the Immaculate Conception and Virgin Birth became everyday miracles. Conceived without sin, woman could represent in 19th century ideology unfallen humanity, that ideal essence of humanity that was to inspire men and uplift them from the sordid world of material getting and spending. Although the mother of many children she was innocent of her own biology and was incapable of participating in or feeling sexual pleasure. Sexuality became exclusively the male sphere, a sign of his more brutish nature, whereas pure womanhood could serve only as a passive vehicle of male sexual pleasure. The very fact that children were produced by sexual intercourse between the parents became the well-concealed scandal of every Victorian household.

This conspiracy of sexual innocence in the bourgeois home governed the conditioning of the female mind and the upbringing of children. Women were swathed in garments that made them unrecognizable as two-legged creatures, and even the legs of furniture were clothed in petticoats to conceal their shocking similarity to human limbs. No bodily organ or function could be even known, much less mentioned, in polite society. Women were shaped to be the walking ideologies of this bourgeois society: half angel, half idiot. Middle-class women were forced into a stifled and sedentary existence. Any kind of physical education or even vigorous movement was impossible. Women were kept in repressed ignorance of their own biology and bodily functions. Hygiene and dietary knowledge were rudimentary. The result was a breed of women prone to sickness who could not easily withstand even the normal rigors of childbearing and household duties. Their life style made many women, including some of the most illustrious who struggled against these myths, quasi-invalids for most of their lives. That women were physically too weak for any vigorous activity became an assumption that created its own fulfillment. Even in the early 20th century it was still widely assumed that vigorous activity and excessive "brainwork" would so exhaust woman's limited vitality that she would be rendered sterile. Higher education for women was widely opposed on these grounds. In 1830 a clergyman educator could confidently declare:

> As for the training of young ladies through a long intellectual course, as we do young men it can never be done. They will die in the process. . . . In forcing the intellect of woman beyond what her physical organization can bear . . . in these years the poor thing has her brain crowded with history and grammar, arithmetic, geography, natural history, chemistry, physiology, physics, astronomy, rhetoric, natural and moral philosophy, metaphysics, French, often German, Latin, perhaps Greek, reading, spelling, committing poetry, writing compositions, drawing, painting, etc., etc. *ad infinitum.* Then, out of school hours from three to six hours of severe toil at the piano. She must be on the strain all the school hours, study in the evening till her eyes ache, her brain whirls, her spine yields and gives way, and she comes through the process of education enervated, feeble, without courage or vigor. Alas, must we crowd education upon our daughters and, for the sake of having them "intellectual" make them puny, nervous, their whole earthly existence a struggle between life and death?[1]

By 1900 these views were no longer defensible. Better diet, more sensible clothes, the ability of women in the elite women's colleges of the east coast to emulate classical university education with equal success would appear to have refuted these dire warnings. Nevertheless a prominent educator in 1903 could still snap waspishly:

> The first danger to a woman is over brain-work. It affects that part of her organism which is sacred to heredity.[2]

Educators such as Sidney Hall, president of Clark University (the man responsible for bringing Freud to America), warned that the education and emancipation of women threatened the physical end of the human race.[3] It was in this atmosphere that Protestant reformers passed severe laws prohibiting the distribution of birth-control information. To combat the tide of dangerous new opinions, a holiday celebrating traditional motherhood was sponsored by Protestant churches in the early 20th century and was soon established as a national holiday.

This ideology of true womanhood, of which the 20th century feminine mystique is a linear descendent, played a crucial compensatory role in the new industrial society that was being formed. Although building upon earlier Mariology and the cult of courtly love, it arose in its 19th-century form as a part of the Romantic reaction against revolution, industrialism and their attendant threats to traditional values. The home and womanhood were to be everything this modern industrial world was not; they were to compensate for everything threatened by the changes in public relations. Here in the home, patriarchy and the rights of birth still held sway as the natural aristocracy even though this concept was everywhere else overthrown in democratic politics. Here the childhood world of fixed certainties could be maintained in a modern world of scepticism. Here emotionality and intimacy held sway in a world dominated outside by unfeeling technological rationality. Here sublimated spirituality combatted the crude materialism of industrial competition. Here an island of beauty, trees and flowers was walled off from the ugly world of factories. Here voluntarism and personalism reigned against an alienated world where men were the cogs in the machine of an impersonal universe. Above all the home was the realm of piety and nostalgic religiosity cultivated by women to which men repaired to comfort their spirits against the insecurity of a new world governed by scientific rationality that left little place for the old faith.

Women were the high priestesses of this atavistic world of the home, the bulwark against industrial society. Women were to be above all religious, to nurture faith in a religion in which men no longer believed but wished to believe that they still believed. They were both the incarnation and the dispensers of that tranquilizing religiousness that Karl Marx called the opiate of the people but which the bourgeois voluntarily imbibed to inoculate themselves against the threatening world of insecurity, doubt, anomie and social restiveness. This demanded that women remain pre-critical and incapable of sharing the world of rational culture that was eroding these certainties. For a woman to become intellectual and sceptical in this way was a shocking rebellion against all that was holy. An irreligious woman was a moral monster.

But woman was not only the chief "tranquilized tranquilizer." She took on the dimensions of a kind of deity in 19th century thought. It became common to speak of the home as a shrine and of woman as a goddess enshrined therein. As Comte puts it in his glowing vision of the future industrial society:

> Positivism encourages the full and systematic expression of feelings of Veneration for Woman . . . Born to love and to be loved, relieved from the burdens of practical life, free in the sacred retirement of their homes, the women of the West will receive from Positivists the tribute of deep and sincere admiration which their life inspires. They will feel no scruple in accepting their position as spontaneous priestesses of Humanity . . . From Childhood each will be taught to regard their sex as the principal source of happiness and improvement . . . Men in all the vigor of their energies, feeling themselves the masters of the Known world, will feel it their highest happiness to submit with gratitude to the beneficent power of womanly sympathy. In a word, Man in these days will kneel to Woman and to Woman alone.[4]

In 19th-century ideology, womanhood took the place of Christ as the symbol of the cult of humanity. The religion of that liberal theology was that of:

> God-manhood or the idealized essence of man. But if the male comes

to see himself as too divided for this role, he puts forth woman as the symbol of this idealized essence of unfallen human nature. In late medieval nominalist theology the Immaculate Conception of Mary made the Mother of God the symbol of *natura pura* or that original, good created nature of humanity preserved from all taint of sin.[4]

This mariological doctrine of *natura pura* somehow became generalized in the 19th century. True womanhood became the theological symbol of *natura pura*.

    This idealization of woman as effectively removed her from the real world of men and public power as had her earlier denigration. It was said that women were too pure, too noble to descend into the base world of public business. To step out of her moral shrine in the home in order to vote, to work, to campaign, all this would sully her virtue and remove from her that veneration that she was accorded in her sequestered role in the home. This "down from the pedestal" argument became the chief tool by which social conservatives in church and society rebutted every effort of the new women's movement to break out of the home. It was used to refute every woman's issue from legal rights to education to suffrage. It illustrates the fundamental ambiguity of the male ideology of "femininity." These characteristics were seen simultaneously as unchangeably rooted in woman's biological "nature" and yet something that would be "lost" instantly simply by her stepping out of her assigned social sphere. Early in this century the Catholic bishops of the United States put themselves solidly on record against women's suffrage. An interview with Cardinal Gibbons illustrates the character of this line of argument:

"Woman suffrage?" questioned the cardinal. . . . "I am surprised that any one should ask the question. I have but one answer to such a question, and that is that I am unalterably opposed to woman's suffrage, always have been, and always will be. . . . Why should a woman lower herself to sordid politics? Why should a woman leave her home and go into the street to play the game of politics? Why should she long to come into contact with men at the polling places? Why should she long to rub elbows with men who are her inferiors intellectually and morally? Why should a woman long to go into the streets and leave behind her happy home, her children, a husband and everything that goes to make up ideal domestic life? . . . When a woman enters the political arena she goes outside the sphere for which she was intended. She gains nothing by that journey. On the other hand, she loses the exclusiveness, respect, and dignity to which she is entitled in her home.

Who wants to see a woman standing around the polling places; speaking to a crowd on the street corner; pleading with those in attendance at a political meeting? Certainly such a sight would not be relished by her husband or by her children. Must the child, returning from school, go to the polls to find his mother? Must the husband, returning from work, go to the polls to find his wife, soliciting votes from this man or that. . . ? . . . Woman is queen," said the cardinal in bringing the interview to a close, "but her kingdom is the domestic kingdom."[5]

Through sneaking innuendo the cardinal contrived to make voting sound like a full-time occupation and exercising the franchise in the American democracy sound like a form of prostitution. The message was clear: for woman to function outside the "sanctuary" of her home was tantamount to becoming a "fallen woman." This idealization of woman also defined her as a being who existed to nurture morality and spirituality in others through the family. Her whole being was that of a "being-for-others." This doctrine was so taken for granted that Auguste Comte could elevate it to woman's chief contribution to the coming positivist society. For Comte this did not mean that woman would exercise any political role directly, only that she would be enshrined in the home as the symbol of the "principle of sympathy." Woman was the heart of society as man was the head. But, as much as the Catholic cardinal, Comte wished her to exercise this "queendom" solely within the domestic circle.[6]

To assert that a woman was in any way a self-defining person who had a being for herself, a self of her own to fulfill, was an unspeakable heresy for the cult of true womanhood. When Nora left her husband in Ibsen's play, *A Doll's House*, declaring that she had an autonomous self to fulfill, the sound reverberated throughout the house of Victorian society. Feminists in England were even called "Ibsenites." Woman's being was essentially that of sympathy, service, self-giving, just as the male was the autonomous self-defining, active self. Superior in love and virtue, it was equally sure that she was naturally inferior in the ability to think or exercise her will. Her moral superiority was freely conceded and even divinized but only in an auxiliary relation to an autonomy defined as exclusively male. Woman existed to "elevate" the male to these higher feelings, but she "elevated" only by remaining totally submissive and self-giving and purged of all self-will. As the *Young Lady's Book* summarized the virtues of women:

> It is certain that, in whatever situation a woman's life is placed from her cradle to her grave, a spirit of obedience and submission, pliability of temper and humility of mind are required of her.[7]

Because these virtues of humility and submission had been viewed as the highest virtues, the "Christian virtues," Christian virtue came to be seen as peculiarly or inherently feminine, and this morality of obedience and humility was exercised only to complement the domination and aggressiveness of men, not to judge them. Christian humility bent into a slave ethic, exercised by those already humbled and not a rebuke to the proud. Again this language revealed the cult of true womanhood as a secular Mariology. Every woman might be the Virgin Mother elevating crude male vigor to higher purity and delicate emotions precisely to the extent that she herself abnegated her will completely to that of the patriarch. Like her archetype she is to repeat endlessly to her "makers": "be it done to me according to thy will." The role of religion was not lost upon her mentors as the chief force for inculcating this desirable mentality. As Caleb Atwala, another preacher of feminine virtue, writes:

> Religion is exactly what a woman needs, for it gives her that dignity which best suits her dependency.[8]

This idealized and privatized sphere of feminine virtue in the home functioned as the antithesis and bulwark against the "real world," which now became defined exclusively by material values. A peculiar reversal of the traditional dualism of male spirit and female "carnality" occurred. In 19th-century ideology, the male world now became "the material world." But this material world was also understood to be the "real world," the world of hard practical aggressivity devoid of sentiment or moralizing. This male world was still the realm of the intellect. But this was reduced to cause and effect rationality and lost the feminine quality of wisdom. This was the work-a-day world of the Victorian male from which he repaired to the idealized world of the "home," where all moral and spiritual values were confined. This split between the public realm of work as the sphere of material relations and functional rationality and the "home" as the feminine sphere of morality and sentiment had a devastating effect on both women and the quality of public culture. Not only did this new schizophrenia forge new arguments to forbid women from stepping outside the home, but it also diverted women's education into those humanistic spheres that both unfit them and gave them little inclination to compete in this type of male world.

On the other hand moral virtues were sentimentalized and privatized, so they ceased to have serious public power. The feminizing of Jesus, which was typical of 19th-century imagery, and the segregation of religion in the suburban sector both reflect the retreat of religion to the home. Even humanistic education and the arts began to suffer the same fate of privatization, while the world of business and government was given over to a technological rationality.

This split between rationality and morality, fact and value, was unwittingly expressed in Reinhold Niebuhr's antithesis between "moral man" and "immoral society." Altruistic morality belongs to the private sphere. It is appropriate only to person-to-person relations exemplified by marriage. In the world of politics and business much morality is "unrealistic." Here the limits of justice are found in the balancing of the clash of competitive egoism. Women are the symbol of the private sphere of love; they exemplify "moral man." Women are moral and men are rational in a way that is emptied of morality. Morality becomes sentimentalized, privatized and identified with the feminine sphere of the home. Those who try to apply such moral judgments to politics and business are unrealistic, sentimental and untimately "effete," that is, "effeminate." Bomber pilots who have no sentimental scruples about "doing their job" are "manly," while those who suffer imprisonment or exile for conscience are "effete." Eugene Bianchi, in the next essay, analyses this masculine definition of the world of public power in our society.

The Victorian cult of true womanhood was clearly a class ideal. In its image of the delicate woman who belonged in the home it studiously ignored the fact that large numbers of poor women were working inhuman hours in factories for pitiable wages. Its sublimated leisure culture for the affluent bourgeois lady was built on a world of repression, both sexual repression that found its outlet in a proliferation of houses of prostitution and the repression of the working class, whose exploited labor was the underpinning of middle-class society. This lower class was viewed as a world of bestial appetites and irrational mob instincts. All the sentimental efforts to restore traditional ruling-class values ultimately aimed at keeping this lower world in its place. These two forms of repression intermingled because the poor woman who could scarcely survive on the wages of the factory often turned to prostitution. Because the cult of true womanhood made the leisured bourgeois woman normative, the plight of working women could be viewed only as a downfall from the sanctity of the home. Its true character as the underside of Victorian repression and exploitation went unnoticed.

By the turn of the century the contradiction between an intensified domesticity and a sexually repressive culture became so violent that the underside of Victorian society exploded in the Freudian revolution. At first Freudian revelations about the repressed sexuality that was the underside of Victorian "purity" were regarded as a great threat to home and womanhood. The age of the "flapper" was a social revolt against the heritage that denied sexual experience to middle-class women. But the sexual revolution in the United States was soon reintegrated into the psychology of the bourgeois family as an integral part of its maintenance. The sexual revolution corresponded to the transformation of capitalism from its earlier sexually repressive work ethic to consumerism. The eroticization of the home and the private sector of life generally became quickly harnessed to consumer capitalism to stimulate its chief function as the primary consumer unit. Women became the chief buyers and the sexual image through which the appetites of consumption are to be stimulated to buy the products of consumer society. Women become a kind of self-alienated "beautiful object" who sell consumer goods to themselves through the medium of their own sexual image. The home becomes the voracious mouth to be stimulated by every sensual image to devour the rapidly obsolescent products of consumer capitalism.

The eroticization of the home and leisure life is also stimulated in capitalist society to compensate for and pacify the alienation of work and the loss of control over public political and economic processes. Women must be kept in the world of leisure culture all the more to service this need for pacification of work alienation. Women become not only the housekeeper and child nurturer but the ideal friend and sexual playmate who appeases the bruised spirits of the frustrated male returning from work.

In the light of this compensatory use of the home, leisure, women and sexuality, we must ask ourselves seriously about the real meaning of that so-called quest for intimacy that grows all the more insistent in modern American life. Is the great burgeoning of encounter groups, of increased sexual frankness, of increasing preoccupation with the private sphere of deep interpersonal relations that is so often fixated on heightened sexual expression a quest that not only is not forbidden but is actively encouraged and even financed by churches, big business and even "enlightened" government agencies? Is this really a part of the solution to a more humanized modern life, or is this not an integral part of the pacification of alienated work and political relationships that sends us on an increasingly obsessive search for compensation in our private interpersonal lives? Above all does the encounter culture and its cult of freer sexuality offer any genuine liberation to women, or is it not a retooling of their roles as sexual pacifiers all the more? Is it not notable that the world of encounter groups and the psychology on which it is based, like the earlier types of psychotherapy, are fundamentally built on male sexism? Women's segregation from active leadership roles is thus reinforced all the more so that she may serve in ever heightened form this compensatory realm of private emotional release. I suggest that as long as the quest for intimacy goes on primarily as private leisure culture it is a part of the sickness of our society and not a part of the solution. The true intimacy of dignified human beings should be the intimacy that goes on not in an escapist flight from the real world of alienated work and power but in the disciplined struggle of men and women together to criticize these false antitheses, to overthrow the walls between personal values and public culture and to build a new human world.

Notes: Chapter III

1. Rev. John Todd, "Lob-Sided," quoted in Thomas Woody, *A History of Women's Education in the United States*; *see* Rosemary Ruether, "Are Women's Colleges Obsolete?", *Critic*, (Oct.-Nov., 1968), pp. 58-64.

2. *N.E.A. Proceedings* (1903), p. 460 (see article by Ruether, above).

3. G. Stanley Hall, *Adolescence*. New York: D. Appleton and Co., 1904, II, 572-92. See Dorothy Fraser, "The Feminine Mystique, 1870-1910," *Union Seminary Quarterly Review*, XXVII/4 (Summer, 1972), p. 229.

4. Heiko Obermann, *The Harvest of Medieval Theology*: Cambridge, Mass., Harvard University Press, 1963, ch. 6.

5. See Documents of the Catholic Bishops against Women's Suffrage, 1910-1920, Sophia Smith Collection. Smith College.

6. Auguste Comte, *A General View of Positivism*. Paris, 1848, ch. 6.

7. *The Young Lady's Book*, New York, 1830, American Edition, p. 28; cited in Barbara Welter, "The Cult of True Womanhood, 1820-1860," *American Quarterly* 18 (Summer, 1966), p. 133.

8. "Female Education," *Ladies' Repository and Gatherings of the West* I (Cincinnati), 12; cited in Barbara Welter.

Chapter IV

The Super-Bowl Culture
of Male Violence

Eugene C. Bianchi

A few years ago I wrote an article[1] claiming that big-time football mirrored in a ritual way some of the worst characteristics of our culture. I argued that the roots of America's penchant for domestic and foreign violence could be found in symbolic and reinforcing ways in the great national sport that preoccupied a significant percentage of our population. My analysis of professional football underlined four qualities that linked to drive the American violence machine: physical brutality, profit-maximizing commercialism, an authoritarian/military mentality and sexism. Of course I was focusing intentionally on the destructive elements of that game; I was not condemning sport in general.

But after two years of reflection I would make only one important change in the earlier perspective: that the fundamental evil from which the others flowed is sexism. The way by which males in our culture establish their sexual identities within themselves and against women is a prime source for exaggerated aggression in the interpersonal, economic and political realms. The problem can be put as follows: How are we conditioned as males in society to value ourselves as persons? What are the criteria of self-worth and social acceptance among American men? I would like to explore these questions in the context of major social institutions and patterns. I am convinced that the answers to the above queries manifest a close relationship between violence and sexism.

Let me enter a brief preliminary word about my use of the terms "violence" and "sexism." I will employ the words "aggression" and "violence" to mean not only destructive conduct towards persons and property; these words also refer to the more subtle types of violence, called avoidable injury or institutionalized violence, that deprive people of rights and resources. By "sexism" I am talking about a learned pattern of relationships among men that creates an adversary and domineering style between males and towards females. These distinctions should become clearer in the examination of concrete social structures and mores.

The American family is the first conditioning agency for the self-identity that leads to aggression. The boy learns very soon that to set out on the journey to real manhood he must perform and compete better than girls, at least physically. It is a tragic experience for a male child to be thought a sissy. He is schooled to muscular and psychic aggressiveness with toys and in games and other exploits denied to girls. He understands from the start that social acceptance of him as a man depends on his being dominant towards and protective of females, while being successfully competitive towards males. The TV show "Sixty Minutes," had a graphic example of such pedagogy lately when it portrayed the indoctrination of youngsters in Midget Football Leagues. Vividly encapsulated in this incident were the parental needs to extend their own competitive/success syndrome through their sons and to ward off fears of "deviant" sexual development in the boys. Toughness, aggression and winning were so highly valued that risk of serious physical injury was minimized to attain those attributes.

The polarization of the sexes is fixed in these childhood activities. Males learn to focus on definite challenges and to overcome them; females begin their schooling in passivity and dependence. Because male-dominant culture needs subservient women, girls are conditioned to suppress their mental and physical potential. Young girls are capable of developing physical expertise and bodily confidence far beyond what they are permitted. Moreover, girls are usually superior to boys of the same age in the mental and verbal skills that could enhance their early physical development. But to form women physically adept and strong would be inconsistent with the derivative functions they are destined to perform in society. As students they would cease being careful but docile notetakers and would exercise critical abilities. As adults they would endanger the structures of patriarchy by expecting to hold leadership positions. Thus the psychosomatic power to challenge must be drilled out of the young girl.

A dual form of subtle violence is at work in these sexist patterns of childhood. Girls are deprived of their rights to develop their psychophysical qualities; later this will breed resentment against male society whether the resentment be consciously articulated or remain an unconscious source of animosity. Secondly, violence is done to the male child by demanding that he conform to the code of toughness and competition. A lifetime of competition among men is destructive to themselves and to other men because it generates self-hatred and an undercurrent of violence in male relationships.[2] Men find it very hard to cultivate a peaceful and accepting self-love in a culture that drives them to achieve impossible and dubious goals at the top of the competitive heap. In an environment of intense competition to dominate in order to establish one's personhood, men must constantly be on guard against their fellows and try to manipulate them for self-advancement.

Another way for children to learn violence in the family is to observe it in father/mother relations. An overt form of violence of men toward women in the home is not a universal phenomenon, but it is a sizable social reality. In addition to wife-beating there are threats of physical force or of abandonment. The last is especially menacing to a woman whose socialization has left her without an independent means of support. She may be punished by being ignored or by having her circle of friends and her movements limited. The young boy observes and incorporates into his own personality these control patterns that can later be used against women. He sees that his father has some power and a public life while his weaker and subordinate mother is confined to submissive and secondary roles. This experience also creates a potentially destructive tension in the male psyche. He may value the unconditional love of the mother while rejecting or even despising her for being reduced to a derivative and dependent status. Later his own desire for position and adventure in the world may cause him to suppress the affectional (mother) dimension in himself to seek power among males.

Feminine resentment at being used and kept in ancillary functions also gives rise to hidden or open hostility in the home. It can result in a psychologically harmful dominance of children who are reared to serve her frustrated needs. Some women take out their resentments on husbands in devious and manipulative ways. These hidden structures of animosity in family life, arising from the sexist framework of our culture, are potent forces for teaching violence. Most of these women are programed from youth to feel unworthy as women unless they are sacrificing themselves for others, a phenomenon that has been aptly termed the compassion trap. They are taught that taking care of their own desires and needs constitutes selfishness. (Christian preaching against self-love has often been couched in a polemic against selfishness, an approach that frequently eliminated the healthy self-love and acceptance necessary for genuine faith.) Women learn from their feminine models that suffering and self-renunciation are the prerequisites for social acceptance as the good wife or mother. Pleasure and self-fulfillment are less worthy, even condemnable pursuits. Ruether (*Sexism and the Theology of Liberation*, p. 11) underlines the importance of self-esteem for women in the process of liberation toward new levels of feminine consciousness.

Society thus emphasizes that female happiness consists of women subordinating their hopes and ambitions to a husband's career, housework and child care. This cultural indoctrination has been all-pervasive and remarkably successful. A sign of its effectiveness is the amount of guilt that women feel when they transgress social norms directing the proper feminine way. Another indication of the success of the training to suffer is the perverted sort of rejoicing in hardship, misery and self-negation that many women manifest. They look for and stress the negative in interpersonal and national happenings as an extension of their own self-negation. Too much happiness depresses them. Yet this widespread cultural style among women also nurtures destructive sentiments that simmer beneath the conventional conduct. The atmosphere created by these resentments becomes one of latent hostility in the family. These unresolved contradictions stimulate superficial and dishonest forms of communication in the household. Joined to feelings of being used or abused, this ambience becomes one of enmity, envy, suspicion and manipulation. These families of noncommunication and inequality provide children with a training ground for violent interactions.

Such a climate can incline a young man to violence by fostering in him a sense of impotence or lack of self-worth because he is forced to exist in a milieu of psychic impotence. The roles and expectations of family members degenerate so that no one can realize personal potential or empower others. When a family becomes a school for impotence it lays the groundwork for violence in a young man. Sociological and psychological studies have related low self-regard to antisocial, aggressive behavior. A sexist family structure can also foster violent leanings in a youth by impairing his power to empathize with others. As a survival mechanism the child may have to deny the reality of hostile and dominative parental relations. Yet such a denial of reality makes it very difficult for a youth to get in touch with his own feelings and wants. The quality of empathy requires the ability to sense our own real feelings for perceiving any pain and hurt we may be causing to others. Persons who commit violent acts against others lack this ability to feel compassion for the pain and terror of the victims.

The fundamental violence-prone sexism of our culture that demands that males compete fiercely to dominate is furthered in school and peergroup relations. What the family began the school promotes in more sophisticated ways. Athletic events, academic grades and examinations are geared to fashion children, especially males, into socially acceptable achievers and competitors. An illuminating corollary to male success education is Matina Horner's study about student women who program themselves to fail in order not to abandon the accepted image of femininity. A humanely competitive attitude is not an inducement to violence. But schools indoctrinate young men with a deadly serious spirit of competition. It is not just a rivalry that helps a person enjoy the contest for the pleasure and skill involved in it; rather it's a confrontation with others in which a man's self-identity, self-respect and public acceptance is at stake. He can hardly afford to lose. Winning is all even if it means trampling on one's fellows. Hostility and violence are instruments for removing obstacles on the road to the top.

The young male psyche is probably more influenced by peer relationships than by formal schooling. Here again peers affect each other from an underlying sexist mentality. Among deprived minority groups the gang phenomenon strongly emphasizes a male-dominant system. The violent patterns in these groups constitute a quick road for a young man to personal selfhood and respect from others. It is a way of becoming a man in a larger society that has stacked the deck against those of minority status. The inclination to violent response is also a survival and protection need for those condemned by the affluent structure to the most vulnerable sector of the population. Aggressive acts help the youth overcome his sense of impotence and insignificance when he is measured by the male norms of the wider culture. A tough stance brings him material rewards, a reputation for bravery and female devotees. The place of women in these groups, as well as in certain alternate life-style arrangements, is essentially subordinate and derivative. She functions to bolster male toughness. Although most of us will not admit it, the gang represents in crude miniature many of the key impulses that drive American society. A national history of aggressive individualism, frontier lawlessness and the glorification of outlaws should make us expect the gang phenomenon. Technology has only helped to update an old American male institution.

The middle- and upper-class male peer group is also a milieu for sexist development. Fraternity hazing is a rite that demands the inflicting of pain to produce real men who can get ahead. This practice declares that for males toughness, not tenderness, must be paramount. The other side of this mentality manifests a proneness to see draft resisters as "faggots" because they refused pain and aggression as an introduction to manhood. Here we are also touching on the terrible fear of homosexuality in a male who is torn between the cultural demand for potency in heterosexual performance and his own fears about his sexual adequacy. The passion for fast cars with unnecessary horsepower is a phallic extension for youths who need reassurance about their sexual manhood. The problem is not that young men are sexually insecure, rather the difficulty and peril consists in the domineering and violence-oriented sexuality that is advocated as a cure to this insecurity. He is encouraged to "score" with girls, to "make" women. The male in this common vision is the individualist hero-hunter who sets out to make a kill, to dominate his prey. It is a sexuality of conquest, of trophies that shine from the inner mantelpiece of his ego.

I affirmed at the outset that the sexism in football was symbolically fundamental to the other evils of our culture. It is also worth noting that in a culture that encourages people to admire and revel in aggressiveness sports of intended brutality gain the highest appeal both at the box office and on television. A prototype of such sport is prizefighting; recent additions to popular games of mayhem are ice hockey and roller derbies. The well-calculated appeal to direct physical abuse in these sports points to the well-instilled need in our people to be entertained by violence. Much of the responsibility for propagating violence-teaching programs rests with the sponsoring corporations that use such programing to sell their products. Yet the high point of violent symbolism in sport is reached in football, which draws the passionate attention of millions. We can focus on that great national pastime as a transition from the male violence among peers to the crimes of men.

Big-time football manifests and reinforces the ideal of masculine

identity through its aggressive ethos. The real man is aggressive and dominant in all situations. The weekend trek to the arena is not an escape from
the world of corporate America; rather it is a weekly pilgrimage to the
national shrines where the virtues of toughness and insensitivity can be
renewed. This is especially true in man/woman relationships. In the football spectacle the role of woman in our society is clearly defined against
the masculine criteria of value. The important action is male-dominated;
women can share only at a distance in a man's world. They can shout and
squeal from afar, but their roles are accessory to the male event. Ultimately they are his "bunnies," his possessions for pleasure and service.

Yet for all its chest-thumping bravado the game also portrays the
anxieties and contradictions of aggressive sexuality. Football, by its very
calculated violence, makes sensitive attunement to one's own body hard to
achieve. The vicious body contact is the opposite of gentle touching and
loving gesture. Moreover, the kind of sexuality implied in the game manifests a fearful displacement of the challenge of sustaining authentically interpersonal sexuality. It is an extension into adulthood of the latency
phenomenon of young boys pummeling each other and avoiding a more
mature relationship with women. Thus the sport depicts an unhealthy
polarity toward women. In one way social canons urge the male to be
dominant and aggressive towards women. Yet in a culture geared to
aggressive attainments men demonstrate a deep fear of delicate, equalitarian sexual relations. Unsure about sexual potency in a milieu that
demands—even in sex—a kind of technological efficiency and performance many men are unable to shake off these cultural imperatives and
relate to women in sex as full equals. With equals there is no need to control the other or to succeed according to external prescriptions.

Violent crimes in the United States are a particularly male phenomenon. Crimes committed by women, however, are on the rise, although
these actions are usually not crimes of direct assault. A combination of
new opportunities for women in the public sphere plus the persistence of
male patterns of competitive gain in the marketplace may partially ex-
plain this increase. Because the statistics on serious crime in our land are
appallingly high in comparison with other nations, we need to ask whether
the formation of the sexist male psyche is involved. The word "crime"
usually conjures up in our minds violence to property (theft) or persons
(assault, homicide). Often, however, we are not subtle enough in imagining
the forms of theft and assault that are peculiar to those in positions of

wealth and power. Watergate and the Pentagon Papers have helped to cure this weakness of the imagination. But for the purpose of my theme, rape provides an unusual way of joining theft and assault while at the same time pointing to the sexist underpinnings of much violent crime. Rape combines a taking away of freedom and other rights as well as the threat or actuality of physical violence. Because the incidences of this kind of violence have been on the rise, the crime merits special attention.

Rape represents a compulsion to dominate and harm women; it also tells us about the mechanisms to perform that obsess men. Rape, often accompanied by physical brutality, manifests a need to control and force a woman to do her attacker's will. This impulse to overpower and coerce is probably stronger than the actual sexual attraction of the act, although the latter is sometimes heightened by the struggle to dominate. The rapist may be venting a rage against his victim that he consciously or unconsciously feels against society or possibly against other women in his life. In this distorted way he is trying to establish his inner sense of power and selfhood against a society that brought him to repeated failures to perform according to its rules and myths. It was Eldridge Cleaver who graphically confessed that in the act of rape, which he later saw as dehumanizing to self and victim, he was striking out against a repressive social order. The rapist may also be demonstrating by displacement an unresolved hatred of, or conflict with, another woman in his life.

Whatever the motives of the rapist the action itself is particularly demeaning for the woman. She is not able to respond as an equal human being because the exchange is based on a man's superior strength or his weapon. Her personal autonomy and individuality are submerged; she is reduced to a thing in a thing-oriented culture. As a subhuman, her terror and pain call forth no empathy. This crime is a culminating point of the cultural formation of the male psyche in terms of the materialistic winner/loser, the hero/hunter whose self-identity depends on performing with things and amassing them. Although we don't want to acknowledge it, rape is the prototype example of the masculine game that pervades society. The competitor, the opponent, the enemy needs to be reduced, humiliated, made powerless, made into woman.

Other social overtones of rape exemplify the violence-prone mentality of our male-dominant society. Fear of such attack is used to perpetuate a status quo where men hold power and women keep their place. The threat of rape fosters the notion that women are like children who need to be protected by male-dominated (and discriminatory) laws and institutions. Women are thereby subtly warned not to branch out too boldly into careers and activities in ways that menace male hegemony. Notice how this message is reflected in the tone of police investigations. By question and innuendo officials shift the blame for the incident to the victim. What was she doing in a certain part of town, why was she dressed provocatively, why was she alone? This kind of interrogation implies that she stepped out of her place in the order of things for which presumption she deserves to be frightened and punished.

The intensity of statutory punishments for rape also have important implications for understanding the male psyche. First, the severity of the sentences makes it less likely that the rapist will be convicted unless he is a member of a minority class, an inferior, already something like a woman. Second, the severe punishment has less to do with concern for woman than with private property. Woman is viewed as the possession of husband or father; an assault on her violates male property rights. This interpretation is corroborated by reviewing the many discriminatory laws against women that restrict her freedom and increase her dependence on male guardians and overseers. The priority of personal-property possession in our culture is further menaced by more direct sexual fantasies and fears when blacks are implicated in raping a white woman. The imagined sexual prowess of the black threatens the white male who has come to believe a legend of his own making.

The male psychic patterns at work in rape are also disclosed, though in more refined and respectable ways, in economic life. I am not only referring to the financial rapaciousness of the criminal underworld, sometimes called the Mafia, but rather to the legal structures and dynamics of our capitalist system where masculine self-identity and value are closely linked to performing according to an intense, competitive code. The motivating ideal of the hero/hunter capitalist is to become worthy by maximizing profits, by amassing ever more wealth. This ideal calls for the virtues of toughness, aggressiveness and a willingness to sacrifice mere humanistic considerations for technological efficiency and material gain. Social concern is largely a hypocritical facade. Exxon and ITT buy humanitarian TV commercials, but the basic ethos of their business is to make the rich richer. The corporation itself is not a community; it exists as an efficiency arrangement to concentrate wealth and power in the hands of a small band of individuals. I submit that the fundamental impulse of our economic system is rapacious at home and abroad because such "rape" fulfills male ego needs conditioned by our culture.

Overt corporate crime is socially harmful behavior by corporations for which the law provides penalties. Many of these activities revolve around the violation of laws governing restraint of trade, anti-trust arrangements, misrepresentation in advertising, fair labor practices, rebates, financial fraud and similar categories. Even a cursory reading of the history of corporate crime indicates how vast and pervasive this phenomenon is in national life. These white collar crimes, usually committed by men, are often not discoverable without extensive investigation, whereas the misdeeds of the poor are found out quickly and publicized. Moreover, the resources of corporations make it possible for them to afford the best legal protection. These imbalances in our system of justice stand out starkly in contrast to the heavy penalties imposed on overt, physical acts of violence and the light sentences handed down for convictions concerning white collar crimes of privileged citizens. These reactions of the courts are partially explained by the intense fear inspired by crimes of direct physical violence, whereas the "clean" crimes of respectable businessmen and politicians generate less emotional response in the populace. But the matter of unfair treatment in the courts is further complicated by racism, dislike for the poor and a willingness to treat kindly men who conform to respectable middle-class conventions. Yet such men of the corporate marketplace are more easily corrupted by the difficulty of assuming personal responsibility in a collective situation. The corporation diffuses responsibility among many persons so that actions are separated from conscientious decision. The result of these crimes in male-dominated corporations is violence done to the environment and the general welfare of the people.

This male marketplace of injustice and inequality that oppresses the many and benefits the few is a breeding ground for violence. The concentration of economic power in relatively few super-corporations means that a very small group of stockholders and managers will accrue vast profits and be in a privileged position to influence public policy. The largest corporations—banks, insurance companies and utilities—are not only able to control competition, they also use their great potential for lobbying and for other forms of political influence to neutralize government regulatory agencies originally established to moderate these massive businesses. Often enough the regulatory agencies themselves become servants of private privilege rather than of the common interest. The power of special interest groups over the state is especially evident in our unjustly regressive tax system. Persons at the lower end of the income scale pay a far greater proportion of their earnings in taxes than do those at the top. Capital gains, depletion allowances, tax shelters and many other deductions favor the rich, while the poor and those of modest incomes are saddled with a cluster of regressive taxes.

All of these basically unfair concentrations of power and perquisites have an important bearing on social violence. This masculine world, created and perpetuated by the ego needs of the male psyche, causes resentment and stress. Sometimes this pressure is only vaguely felt and understood although it causes an undefined malaise and frustration, a sense of being driven by uncontrollable outside forces. These stresses of the corporate marketplace adversely affect the lives of those who derive the greatest material benefit from it. But, for successful men, the marketplace is a competitive compulsion, an arena for conquest and ego enhancement, however much it stunts their growth as persons. The poor and the economically marginal tend to see society as hostile and manipulative, as a milieu that offers small hope for their betterment. This attitude is especially violence-prone in deprived racial and ethnic groups. A kind of undirected rage stemming from self-hatred and resentment towards society can be turned inward or outward. Such persons do violence to themselves through drugs and alcohol; at times they strike out in anti-social acts of vandalism and crime. When these sentiments of bitterness towards unjust social structures are illumined by a meaningful rationale, channeled by organization and inspired by leadership, the possibilities of civil rebellion increase. Such resistance and revolt against the status quo frequently goes beyond nonviolent protest to planned tactics of violence. Long-accepted structures of injustice therefore can eventually become the major causes of personal and social violence.

A major reason for maintaining this inequitable economic order is that a man's sense of masculinity is intimately linked in our culture to his ability to make money. The vast majority of Americans still judge a man successful and thus a worthy human person by the amount of money he gathers. Certainly, the movements and alternative life styles of the last decade have questioned this economic determinant of virility.

But it would be a mistake to exaggerate the effectiveness of hippie and New Left influences. Few, even among the young, have been affected beyond the veneer of clothing, hair styles and musical tastes. Can anyone who works on a college campus today seriously believe that America has been greened? To expect such a change of heart would be to deal in what Dietrich Bonhoeffer called "cheap grace." The insecurities and ego requirements of men still attach success and sexiness to making lots of money. Wealth in our system is the leverage of public power and private significance. Its acquisition prompts men to violent strivings; its loss sometimes leads to suicide. When the center of life is gone, why go on?

When women struggle for or attain equal financial standing with men, men feel castrated. On the flip side of this economic scenario, males have protected their money/identity prominence by using women as cheap labor while mouthing their self-serving ideology about mother and home. The first step towards wisdom would be to own up to the intrinsic rapaciousness of an economic system that serves male power needs (not the healthy and humane growth of men) while it keeps women in a deprived and subservient position. There is little chance that we will reform seriously our all-controlling economic system unless we dwell and act on the awareness that it is permeated with a sexist violence. The system demands that women be "scripted" for nurturing and support roles while men be destined to realize their worth through money and power. Unfortunately, it is also a structure that keeps men from fostering lives of intimacy and community, and it even prevents them from finding real pleasure in work itself.

More women now perceive the importance of attaining some economic independence from men. This freedom allows them to overcome the frustrations of an adult constrained into childlike dependency. It also promotes maturity and self-determination in making choices about the disposition of one's own resources. Some critics of woman's newly achieved economic independence claim that it will simply lead them into the same destructive paths of capitalist competition that afflict men. While the danger of such entrapment is real, women must live in an economic system that will not readily change for the foreseeable future. It is in that milieu that women are destined to benefit from whatever self-determining potential such financial independence can give. If women in pursuit of monetary self-sufficiency do not jettison the humanizing qualities learned by their gender over the centuries they may avoid the worse aspects of male economic violence and may bring a new and less avaricious spirit to the marketplace. Male critics of economic independence for women also fear the challenge to the traditional masculine ego of the provider. But men need not suffer ego loss if they learn to look at the positive benefits to them of female economic independence.

The education of the male mind through the social institutions considered has prospects on the political level that are frightening for our national political structures and also for human survival. The familiar slogans of not negotiating on our knees in Vietnam, of not turning tail, of being Number One, of not presiding over the first American defeat are the proud shouts of little boys who learned that winning was all. The culture of the "fastest gun" and of Bonnie and Clyde has a ready penchant for the quick trigger finger. No one has ever lost his job on the National Security Council for being tough—only for being soft on enemies. This code of toughness views the international political scene as a game board for power manipulations, for keeping control, for placating the male psyche.

At home the code of toughness decrees that men should attain power by any means available. This is the real message of Watergate. Notice also that Watergate was a male-only phenomenon. When a woman finally appeared among the conspirators, she was a secretary who bungled a tape-recorder. But the ethic of Watergate is that it's all right if one doesn't get caught. It's also the individualist ethic of the American hero/hunter: power for our side means there's something in it for me; I will become more important through this power-grab. Yet this power of violence destroys the power of democracy that depends on justice and open consensus. Again the lesson is that the Watergate lads (and they are symbols for many others) are living in fundamental contradiction to the best in the American heritage. But such men are acting in full accord with their training in the super-bowl culture of male violence.

As Robert N. Bellah has pointed out in his work on civil religion in America, the political structure of the nation has long experienced the tension between utilitarian and communitarian impulses. The utilitarian principle, classically stated by Hobbes in its most pessimistic and malevolent form, affirms that society is based solely on the pursuit of individual self-interest. Locke modified the principle in somewhat more positive directions with his theory of social contract, and a distorted development of Calvinism was used to bless individual gain. In politics this now dominant philosophy leads to lust for power at the expense of justice. The Lockean social contract is interpreted as merely the framework for fostering private wealth and power. A secularized Calvinism gives respectability to the ethic of amassing wealth individually. Men show the signs of salvation through advanced accumulation and consumerism; they manifest the signs of righteousness through exercising power over others. This pragmatic and individualist principle is seen in our culture as the only way to security in a precarious existence. This guiding theory, which holds almost undisputed sway in the male mind, nourishes the taproot of personal and social violence. Its premise is that humans are ever tending towards the war of all against all. In this dangerous jungle, life's goal is to protect and enhance the self through wealth and influence. For those caught up in these pursuits, the structure and rhetoric of democracy provide a convenient mask for the real aim of the individualist hero/hunter: his own aggrandizement.

Yet the communitarian ethos, which Rosemary Ruether discusses in the context of sisterhood (Chapter III), also struggles for its humanizing place on the polarized scene of American life. The founding doctrines of the nation stress the common welfare as a chief end in itself. The ideals of political checks and balances, of equality before the law, of civic and social freedoms rest on the presupposition that benevolent community is possible, necessary and eminently desirable. In the Western religious perspective, the good political community is akin to the community of charity. This means life lived in trusting, sharing, caring communities. The nation's founders, many of whom held to an Enlightenment, humanistic version of the religious ideal, intended to place the common weal ahead of individualism. In such an assessment there is no need to deny the bourgeois and privatized dimensions of the philosophies and life styles of men like Jefferson, Madison and Monroe. One could even conclude that the degree of individualism cultivated in the 18th century would be detrimental in contemporary circumstances. But the insights and convictions about life, liberty and the pursuit of happiness implied at root a communitarian outlook. This ideal has largely been lost in our culture; utilitarian individualism prevails everywhere. If communitarian theories and ways of life could permeate the spheres of education, work and personal relations, then violence in our society would diminish greatly. Men would not need to prey on one another to assure self-esteem and material security.

The American male mystique is not only opposed to the best elements of the Bill of Rights and the Declaration of Independence, it is also a rejection of the core ethos of the Judeo-Christian tradition. For our future national destiny, the violence-prone male mentality promises constant opposition to qualities that promote the common welfare of justice, equality and community. In the Western religious tradition the masculine mystique is a denial of essential biblical perspectives. I would like to contrast these opposed orientations without further elaboration in this presentation.[3]

The Gospel way stresses the building of trusting life-supporting communities; the male mystique emphasizes individualist self-aggrandizement through the domination of others. The Scriptures advocate the sharing of resources, the hero/hunter mentality nourishes itself by amassing and quantifying things for the self or its immediate extensions. The biblical way points to a democratic communion of persons who share their gifts with one another; the super-bowl psyche inclines men to concentrate political power and decision-making in the hands of the dominating few. Finally, the male mystique is geared towards overt and hidden forms of violence, whereas the Judeo-Christian ideal evolved toward an ethic of minimizing destructive aggression. Unless we are willing to see and deal with these contradictions we continue to live with a false conscience that is psychologically and spiritually damaging. It would be a purist mistake to think that any of us can live in this society without some complicity in its evil tendencies and actions. It is quite another matter to blind ourselves to hypocritical contradictions and even claim that they are glorious virtues.

I have intentionally reviewed the male mystique of violence in the context of our social/cultural conditioning. My purpose is to emphasize that spiritual growth and theological reflection are intrinsically related to the worldly process of becoming freer of personal and social oppressions. The focus of Hebrew and Christian Scriptures is the process of liberation from bondage, from the powers of death that diminish our humanity. The prototype of our enslavements is the oppression of women. From this primal distortion of the male mind proceeds the oppression of other "lesser people." The conquering needs of the violence-prone masculine psyche drives us to racism, colonialism and other types of imperialism. These oppressions are extensions of the male/female pattern by which we project the dark side of ourselves on to the other in order to use and abuse our fellow for our own selfish aggrandizement. Of course, women, too, can imitate the same life style and reproduce its oppression, but this would demand a greater and more difficult rejection of qualities that women have long preserved in our culture.

At root, male chauvinism is a denial of our co-humanity with others and also a rejection of the masculine (*animus*) and feminine (*anima*) within all of us as individuals. My intention in affirming this is not to berate men but hopefully to aid them to see that the male mystique is also the instrument of our own bondage. It keeps us from realizing our full personhood because the oppressor is also oppressed. As American men we are deeply conditioned from the cradle to value ourselves as persons according to the hero/hunter myth of aggressive individualism. How can we change the basic myth by which we live? How can we begin to sense our self-worth according to another model, that of affectionate, nondominative, sharing, communal men? On our own answers to these questions depend the survival of humanity and the restoration of our own personal humanity.

Notes: Chapter IV

1. Eugene Bianchi, "Pigskin Piety," *Christianity and Crisis*, February 21, 1972, pp. 31-34.

2. Joseph Pleck, "My Male Sex Role—And Ours," *Win*, April 11, 1974, pp. 8-12.

3. Eugene C. Bianchi, "Capitalism and Christianity Revisited," *The Christian Century*, December 6, 1972, pp. 1241-44.

Chapter V

The Personalization of Sexuality

Rosemary Ruether

Why is it that cultures, especially those that regard themselves as refined, have tended to depersonalize and brutalize sexuality? Sigmund Freud noted this in an essay entitled "On the Universal Tendency to Debasement in the Sphere of Love." He believed that culture creates a split between the tender, affectionate feelings and the sensual feelings, making it impossible to be fully sensual with those whom one respects, while making it necessary to degrade socially and morally those with whom one permits oneself free sensual activity. Freud held out little hope that this tendency could be overcome. For him sexual intercourse and the genitals were intrinsically disgusting and bestial to refined tastes, and so the tendency to split sensual from humane feelings was an almost inevitable casualty of culture. He notes curiously that this tendency appears primarily in men. Women have little tendency to debase men in the act of love "because they don't bring to the act the same over self-esteem."[1]

As a Catholic child I was given two contradictory messages about sexual love. *Qua* sex this instinct was supposed to be spurned as a bestial force. Every effort had to be made to repress it and to shrink from it in horror. As something called "love" within marriage it became highly idealized, but only to the extent that its bodily side was no longer mentioned. "Love" took place among angels in heaven; sex took place in the gutter. The human level was missed. The root of this great fear of sexual feeling in our culture, which has wasted so much of our moral energies, somehow puzzled me. The explanations about why this was "bad" somehow failed to convince me.

What does the fear of sexuality really represent? Are we really so afraid of our own bodies? Are men that afraid of women? If women are free to be sexual, are men afraid that they will be exposed as less competent? Why has sexual feeling been treated as a "threat from below" that will destroy the mental and moral self? Freud, as much as Christian puritanism, has presented sexuality in that way. Sexual feeling is seen as the bestial self, both an animal and an evil power that must be repressed and controlled so that intellect, virtue and spirit can rise. For Freud too sexual repression is the necessary price that must be paid for the emergence of culture. Few moralists have ventured the contrary view of this assumption represented by William Morris' declaration that "if we feel the least degradation in being amorous, or merry, or hungry, or sleepy, we are so far bad animals and therefore miserable men."[2]

Recently I have come to suspect that the splitting of sex and love for the sake of enobling "love" and "respect for women" is really a cultural lie that covers up what it is that we really fear most. I suspect that what males (who have been the cultural shapers of these attitudes) fear most is not sexual experience but rather ego-vunerability through communication of the inner self. Eugene Bianchi, in the essay that follows this one (ch. 6), has made the intriguing suggestion that even our heterosexual relations are pervaded by what he calls "psychic celibacy." Masculinist society segregates itself from women so profoundly that even in the sexual act it is difficult to express real interpersonalism. The male operates within a self-enclosed world that reduces the woman sexually to a vehicle for himself, rather than being a fellow person. Sex depersonalized allows the male to avoid the challenge of using his total self, uniting energies with personal identities, to present and communicate one to another. Sex has been the victim of the dread of love.

I received a letter recently from a philosopher who had fallen in love for the first time in middle age who said that "men fear love because it is similar to a death experience." Sexual experience somehow was associated with self-loss. Is this fear primarily on the physiological level as some pyschiatrists have claimed—loss of semen, the commitment of the genitals to the woman's body, the flaccid state after intercourse?

Not only modern psychologists but ancient religions have put strange taboos around these physiological effects, even associating withholding of semen with the building-up of vigor in the male. But surely we must see that these physiological effects have been vested with fears on the level of ego-vulnerability and personal commitment that they by no means need to signify. In other words "loss of control" of semen and erection have been vested with a quite different and unrelated "ego-meaning" in the sense of the ability to psychologically detach oneself, distance oneself and continue to dominate the other person. It is this second effect that one really fears. What one wants to do is the first without experiencing the second. One wants the sexual experience to retain its character as an "invasion" in which the invader remains in control and does not himself have to experience any self-surrender. This seems to me peculiarly the male experience of sexuality, while from women's side the opposite is the case. Here one has to deal with a demand for a self-surrender that is debased toward rape rather than opened up as mutual communication. Self-surrender is treated by the male as a threat to control of "his world," rather than a potential release into a larger world than the monistic self. This seems to me to be the dynamics that cause men to hold back from real self-disclosure in sexual experience. The self is split from the body, and the body then can be manipulated as an external instrument of domination in a way that does not threaten to dissolve the defenses of the ego. This kind of sexuality seems to be well-illustrated in the movie "Last Tango in Paris." This kind of sexual experience without self-surrender and disclosure demands, as its complement, the depersonalization or debasement of woman.

The dream of ecstatic love inspires poets. To open oneself to deep vulnerability and communication is profoundly terrifying, especially when it is unified with sexual experience as a total body-potential that transforms communion into ecstasy. In actuality, we shrink from the full possibility of such an experience because it would demand great inward development and openness, a self-searching and self-giving that would find the deepest I-thou at the point where the ego dissolves. This vision of total ecstatic self-giving and communion has dominated religious mysticism, but the mystical tradition separated the inner experience from its sexual foundation and sublimated it into the vision of contemplative ecstasy in quest of God. To recognize that this possibility of love might be expressed in a real relationship with another person would concretize that experience. Sexuality signifies the potential for ecstasy in interpersonal relations, but we betray this possibility through sublimation of our ecstatic powers and depersonalization of our body and that of the other. Sexuality is debased to ward off the challenge of love.

Historically there have been two ways of debasing sexuality—the ascetic and the libertine. The ascetic always accuses his critics of libertinism, but in fact the two are merely two sides of the same split. Not infrequently, as in ancient Gnostic sects or even in medieval culture, the two tended to appear side by side, at least in the tangled accusations and assertions of sectarian polemic.[3] Even conventional ascetic writings, such as those of Bernard of Clairvaux, reveal to what extent the contemplative quest is built on repressed and sublimated eroticism. The ascetic represses physical experience and withdraws in revulsion from his own body and from that of the opposite sex. Ecstasy is to be solely an interior experience between the "bridal soul" and God. Yet it was precisely the erotic language of the ancient Near Eastern marriage poem, the *Song of Songs*, that became the chief biblical text that provided Christian mysticism with the language for the ecstatic communion between the soul and its "divine lover."[4]

In ascetic cultures, sex hardly disappears as a fact of life. But it must be debased into a depersonalized sphere where it can make no spiritual demands. The body is objectified as an alien, dangerous force that must be crushed into submission. What this means is that the realm of bodily experience becomes separated out as a "lower realm" where one might capitulate to this force, but in a way that cannot be integrated into the moral and responsible self. Concubinage for the celibate priest and prostitution for the puritanical Victorians were the "underworld" created to compensate for the work of sublimated idealism.

We must see that a power relationship of supra- and subordination between men and women is essential to this schism of mind and body. Only by making one person in the relationship inferior, dependent and "purely carnal," can one assure a sexuality without the challenge of interpersonalism. By making woman "carnal," one does not have to relate to her as a person. Asceticism does not have the effect of preventing the ascetic from having any sexual experiences. Rather it assures that whatever experiences he has will always be treated as "sin." As soon as one can "gain control" over oneself one should repress this experience, repent and return to sublimated "purity." This is evident in the discipline of celibates in Catholicism now. The Church can forgive the repentant "fornicator." It cannot forgive the man who establishes a responsible human relationship with a woman. This means that the female partner must be identified essentially with sin and treated as a wanton lower being who is to be tossed aside like dirt. Asceticism separates out the love-ecstasy potential of sexuality as something fundamentally alien to the body. It becomes fantasized as a purely interior relationship to be experienced by withdrawing from the evil realm of the body, the woman and the world.

The Victorian era to some extent revolted against this repressive culture but in other ways retained its split between sex and love, now splitting women into sublimated angelic women and debased carnal women. True love was "spiritual" in a way that must repress its bodily reality. "Good women" had to be represented as sexual innocents. Only thus could they serve as the love object of one's dream. At the end of that era there was a revolt against this sublimation of sexuality. Freud to a large extent reversed the process by revealing everything that has been called love as a concealment of purely carnal drives. But the assumption that these carnal drivers were animal in the pejorative sense is still presumed in Freud's demystification of Victorian culture. Materialist anti-Victorianism unmasks the angel to find the animal. Again the human level is missed.

Nevertheless, what has been called the sexual revolution in the 20th century has at least begun a quest to reintegrate mind and body in interpersonal experience. Women began to reclaim their rights to sexual experience, which had been denied them by the Victorian split between idealized love in the family and debased sex in the underworld of the brothel. However, this hope of sexual liberation remains unfulfilled as long as it is not centered on the liberation of the personhood of women. Without that, sexual liberation still remains defined in male terms as a new opportunity for sexual exploitation of women, a general promiscuity that turns middle-class society itself into a brothel. The newly eroticized middle-class woman was quickly co-opted by consumer culture to whet its appetites in a way that reinforces the domestication of women.

Even in the student left and counterculture, presumably in revolt against the hypocrisy of suburban consumer culture, the same view of women as sexual objects prevailed. This was true of the revolutionary youth culture in the early part of the 20th century, as well as in the 1960s. The ambivalence is well-illustrated in the famous dialogue between Lenin and Clara Zetkin on the woman question in 1920.[5] Lenin's paternalism towards women and his Victorian puritanism is evident. Yet he protests against the "glass of water theory" of the young revolutionaries that would reduce sex to a purely physiological impulse that needs to be satisfied without respect to those tender emotions, commitment and personal fidelity that have traditionally gone under the name of love. Radical women in the Sixties also discovered that they had been betrayed into a male-oriented libertinism defined in terms of their willingness to make themselves available for what traditional Christian theology would have called "the relief of concupiscence." The materialist debasing of sex, as much as the ascetic repression of it, reveals the inability to integrate sex and love around authentic interpersonalism.

Such a materialist concept of sexual liberation must inevitably demand a depersonalized and exploitative view of women. However much women are exhorted to learn the same casually physical view of sexual experience, the continued power relations between men and women assure that they will be more the victims in the process. Women found themselves angrily charged with having "hangups" if they wanted their sexual relations to signify personal affection, commitment and communication. They found themselves subjected to an interpretation of sexual liberation that meant physical experience without getting involved. It became apparent that this was possible only by retaining the traditional power relations between men and women—the reduction of women to domestic servants and sexual objects. The New Woman's Movement of the late Sixties grew out of this shock.

The woman's movement today is still confused over the distinction between sexual liberation and women's liberation, especially because the media contrives to identify the second with the first. Women today have little desire to retreat to the stiff celibacy of the first women's movement (although its advantages have become apparent to a few radical women who found their energies becoming consumed by sexual affairs!). Generally women wish to retain their rights to sexual experience gained by the revolt against Victorianism. But they are struggling to discover what developments are necessary to assure the centering of sexual liberation within women's liberation. It is the autonomy, the dignity, the wholeness of the woman as a person that must become the center from which a woman operates sexually, as she operates intellectually, politically or economically. At root this means a struggle to overcome the split between the self and the body, created by male culture, that demands either the repression or sexual exploitation of women. Sexual experience can be reunified with interpersonal communication only when sexual liberation is centered upon the liberation of women.

But the effort in revolutionary culture to liberate sex by making it casually physiological is not that foreign to similar trends going on in mainstream bourgeois culture. Popular American culture holds out a promised land of enhanced sexual expertise and erotic fulfillment as the goal of every well-adjusted suburban couple. To produce bigger and better orgasms is the new way of keeping up with the Jones.' But American married couples grow increasingly disappointed with their sexual lives. This disappointment is treated as a purely mechanical and functional problem. The mass media is glutted with "how to" books on sexual prowess. Sex clinics grow up, where the traditional prostitute is transformed into a therapist to teach the inept how to function better sexually. One such therapist proclaimed in a glossy cover spread on sex clinics in *Time* magazine that "it is just like learning to ride a bicycle. Once you get the knack of it, you never forget it." Sexuality becomes a mechanical skill to be taught so people can get more mileage out of each other as stimulators of orgasmic experience. But this quest for orgasmic experience is steered away from touching the real core of the person. One makes love with genitals, not selves. This reverses the traditional mind/body split but does not alter the split itself. Just as asceticism tried to hang on to a self-enclosed ego by repressing the body as dirty, so sexual liberation seems equally determined to eclipse the mind, the spirit and the person so that people can be liberated to "really feel."

This reversal of asceticism is illustrated in the strange and tragic life of William Reich, a thinker who became the evangelist of revolutionary sexual liberation for the New Left in the 1960s. Few people in this century struggled so deeply with the social implications of sexual repression in Western culture as he. Of all the post-Freudians, he most clearly saw that the fundamental basis of sexual repression is patriarchal power. He sought to convince his comrades in the Marxist Left that sexual liberation was an essential part of a socialist revolution. But in his own way Reich fell victim to the mind/body split of Western culture. Because intellect and culture were the enemies of erotic energy, according to orthodox Freudianism, they have to be eclipsed because only so can one recover one's original unfallen orgasmic powers, repressed by patriarchal civilization.[6]

For Reich this suggested that wholesome sex need not be personal; indeed sex is possible only when this "bourgeois" quest for love is given up. Everyone should be able to make love with everyone without respect to any structure of commitment, personal affection or communication between them. In this restored paradise of pre-patriarchal promiscuity, women as much as men would be able to exercise their sexuality freely.

The search for the resurrected body beneath sexual repression and the rise of consciousness demands a reversal of those traits of consciousness and individual personhood won thereby. In Reich's paradise, bodies could be freed for full orgasmic experience only by remaining nameless and faceless to each other.

Reich ended his life in the federal penitentiary at Lewisberg, Pennsylvania, in 1957 after having been expelled for his radical views by both the Communist party and the International Psychoanalytical Association. In the USA, Reich's sexual experiments were brought to a halt by criminal charges leveled at him by the federal government, accusing him of crossing state lines with intent to defraud. In the heyday of the McCarthyite anti-communist witchhunts there were few to defend a man who was both a Marxist and a sexual eccentric. Reich's "fraud" consisted of his invention of the "orgone box." This was a device that he believed could measure orgasmic energy like electricity. The orgone box represented Reich's search for a sexuality that could be controlled, released and measured like mechanical energy. Just how unrevolutionary such a concept of mechanized sexual energy could be is illustrated by Woody Allen's recent fantasy "Sleeper." In this film the hero is transported to a technological totalitarian society of the future where everyone has been rendered frigid, while their sexual experience is provided for them by hooking up periodically to orgone boxes. In modern technological society the repression of consciousness and the eclipsing of personal autonomy becomes the way of affirming the demands of the body without relationship to the mind. Mind-repression rather than body-repression becomes the new way of avoiding the challenge of love.

Much of the enormous pressure upon modern marriage comes about precisely because demands are being placed upon it today that were never placed upon it before. Moralists for several generations have been wont to bemoan the decline of the family, as though the kind of family living in modern American suburbia had existed since the dawn of history and had only recently begun to fall into trouble. In fact this modern notion of the family is a peculiar product of an evolution that began in the late medieval and Renaissance period and has only recently assumed its present character.

Marriage traditionally was a matter of clan alliances, transmission of property to legitimate heirs and assurance of a legitimate line of descent. It secured the legitimate wife a certain framework of support. There was little attempt until the dawn of modern bourgeois culture to demand a unification of marriage and love. In bourgeois culture also it was assumed that the wife soon became worn out by childbearing and housework and ceased to be an interesting erotic partner. Both sexuality and love interests were sought outside the home. The love for the wife, proclaimed as an ideal, remained little more than a formalized respect with little emotional feedback to the woman. Good Victorian women were supposed to be beyond any need for sexual comfort.

The Freudian revolution eroticized the middle-class wife at the very moment when other classes of women, such as domestic servants, prostitutes, serfs and slaves were being abolished, and to put the burden upon the wife of fulfilling all the functions that had once been carried out by a retinue of socially differentiated women. The suburban housewife is wife and mother, sublimated ego-ideal and sexual companion all rolled together. She must dress like a mistress but do the dirty work of a domestic servant. She must be as stimulating a conversationist as the ladies of the French salons while at the same time she remains confined to a world largely bounded by the supermarket and the nursery. It was this idealization of the all-competent modern woman that was blown apart by Betty Freidan's *Feminine Mystique*, the book which more than any other heralded the restlessness of the suburban wife that preceded the new woman's movement.

Much of the recent thinking on marriage has been an attempt to rethink this fusion of sexual fulfillment, friendship and the maintenance of the domestic support system for child-raising into one all-purpose marriage. The assumption that all these can or should normatively be combined in one totalitarian relationship is again being questioned. Yet it is difficult to know how to separate them in a society that no longer admits of many survivals of secondary classes of women. Prostitutes, weekday mistresses and even some domestic workers still exist of course, but the new speculation does not have to do with restoring this traditional kind of separation of love, sex and procreation, but of discovering new pluralisms that do not depend on that kind of fragmentation and debasement of women into separate service functions for male consumption. The new question is whether women themselves cannot enjoy that kind of plurality of relations without suffering social opprobrium, and how such a possibility relates to the traditional functions of marriage.

Historically, monogamy in patriarchal society has been closely linked with the private property relationship of man over woman. Monogamy was always one-sided, accepting the double standard that bound the wife's sexuality in an exclusive relationship of private possession to the husband but did not similarly bind the husband to exclusive sexual fidelity to the wife. The Church preached reciprocal monogamy but in many ways acceded to the double standard. It continued to be taken for granted, from Augustine to the modern Italian confessor, that prostitutes are necessary to preserve the "honor" of wives. Fidelity of husbands to wives then had less to do with sexual exclusiveness on their part than with provision of material support. It was the wife whose honor and social existence was in jeopardy if she had sexual relations with anyone other than her husband.

Modern romantic marriage not only demands in theory reciprocal sexual exclusivity but life-long companionship, romance and erotic satisfaction. The failure to combine all these roles in one results in "serial monogamy." Each marriage is presumed to be a new attempt to combine friendship, sex and domestic comfort in one exclusive package. But the exclusive packages become increasingly short-term, rather than permanent. A recent article by a marriage counselor-minister in *Christianity and Crisis* attempted to ask whether we haven't lifted up the wrong priority in making sexual exclusivity rather than long term friendship and personal fidelity the chief test in making or breaking monogamy. Perhaps we might even have more long-term fidelity and personal commitment if sexual exclusivity were not made its primary component. What really is the value that society wishes to preserve most? Is it sexual exclusivity, especially when divorce and remarriage turn this into a serial exclusivity? Or is it not long-term commitment, both for personal support and friendship and for secure child-raising that can provide stable parental figures for the new generation?[7]

Sex, friendship and child-raising are falling apart in modern marriage in new ways. This, however, itself does not express some new barbarianism by moderns. Rather it expresses the fact that these three functions have never been easily combined. Traditional societies split them from each other. Classical Christianity split sublimated love and debased sex, but it also accepted *de facto* separations of marriage from sex in secular society. We who have tried to fuse all these functions in one monistic life-long relationship are discovering again the traditional tensions among them. If we seek new pluralisms we do so with new demands—demands that sex be loving and that marriage be sexually fulfilling.

Shall we put down our inability to realize the ideal of romantic marriage to original sin? Certainly elements of sin, in the sense of inability to overcome selfishness and exploitation, play a large role in this failure. But there are also authentic values rather than simply moral turpitude that make the ideal of romantic marriage hard to fulfill. Marriage as an arena of generational identity, personal security and child-raising is intended to be fairly permanent. Children can survive the breakup of households and the inability to relate to both parents as members of the same household. But something in the stability of personal identity is shattered by this. Few people look forward to old age when no structure of personal support has been built up to provide a caring community. These then are the essentials of the family that need to be preserved. But it is questionable whether these functions are best secured when the only bond that holds it together is a highly volatile and changeable sex/love between a couple.

In more traditional extended families, various adults within the familial unit provided a sense of security and a stable structure for child-raising even when the relation of the parents failed. Moreover, the family had a multiplicity of economic functions. It was a little factory, the basic production unit of society. Today the family has lost almost all productive functions and the economic glue that holds it together is often little more than the unskilled character of the wife who is economically dependent on the husband's income to maintain her life style. This thread of economic necessity vanishes when the wife becomes economically self-sufficient. Yet we have hardly overcome our need for family. Indeed, the demand for families simply as places of mutual support seems to be growing apace in those very sectors of society that have tasted a rootless individualism. What we find then is the exploration of new kinds of "tribes" or extended families that can recreate the sense of a stable community for mutual support and child-raising. Here the relationships of couples might go through fluctuations and even separations, but the primary functions of the family can continue to be carried out in and through these fluctuations in personal relations.

If the word family evokes a need for some on-going framework of identity through time, the evolution of personal identity through love relationships seems to demand more plurality than that traditionally allowed in monogamy. Monogamy has especially atrophied the personal development of women who were expected to get their entire emotional feedback through a relationship to a single man while he in turn developed his personality through a multiplicity of friendships, business relationships and even sex relationships. The confining of one's personality development to a single life-long love relationship does not seem to accord with the laws of either personal growth or friendship.

Western philosophical thought seems to have had its greatest difficulty in dealing with finite plurality. But finite plurality is the place of actual human existence. The libertine demands infinite promiscuity, but such totalism, which tries to embrace boundless experiences, can hardly develop into depth relationships. By nature it translates love into a depersonalized sexuality. But the exclusive sex/love ideal is equally totalitarian. It demands a total compatibility of two people; their ability to satisfy each other on every level of personality, intellect, sexuality, and to continue to do so in a static way for a lifetime of marriage. Because no relationship fits that kind of totality we go on an endless search of perfect compatibility. We feel free to break apart relationships that fail to meet our standards. A strong principle of fidelity that committed a couple to particular tasks together would be far preferable, but this assumes that each is an evolving person undergoing stages of growth that demands other relationships, other depth friendships, to nourish emerging potentials of the self. These new relationships might well also return and nourish the primary relationship between the couple as well. In short, what is faddishly called "open marriage," represents a quest for a mature way to form relationships that can combine a more plural sense of friendships for both women and men with more long-term fidelity of married couples to the tasks of community and family building.

The personalization of sexuality challenges both the traditional Christian doctrine that sex be limited to procreation and also the libertine view that reduces sex to physiological relief without depth communication and relationship. If the personalization of sexuality challenges the traditional view that sex can be limited solely to procreative marital acts, it equally challenges the hidden exploitativeness and depersonalism of what passes for sexual liberation. It demands a morality based on the laws of careful friendship that would judge as immoral not only much of what passes for sophisticated liberty in modern society but also much that passed for legitimate married relations in traditional society. It demands that both partners to any relationship look upon each other as beloved persons to whose total welfare and personal growth each is committed. Such a concept does not fit itself easily into traditional laws. It demands a higher, not a lower, standard by which to judge the immorality or morality of sexual relations.

The personalization of sexuality must also throw into question the norm of heterosexuality as the sole norm of healthy sexual relations. The view that made heterosexuality the only legitimate expression of sex/love depended on two assumptions, both of which are challenged by personalized sexuality and the growth of women to autonomy and personhood. The first presupposition is that sexuality is primarily for procreation. Sexual relations must be "oriented to the possibility of procreation," even if every act is not procreative. Sexual communion cannot be viewed as good in itself detached from this procreative end. Hence homosexual love, which is inherently nonprocreative, cannot be either "natural" or "good."

A second more subtle argument against homosexuality lies on the level of what are presumed to be the psychic natures of men and women created by their distinct biologies rather than simply an argument confined to biological procreation. This argument assumes a doctrine of "complementarity." Those traits traditionally called masculine and those called feminine are presumed to define the unchangeable natures of men and women. Men are actors, thinkers, doers who protect and act upon others. Women are passive, dependent, weak in their ability to take care of themselves, emotional, lacking full rationality, perhaps more "spiritual" and "intuitive." Sexuality to be whole must unite these two halves of the human psychophysical essence. Sexual union by nature must be a union of the two opposite sexes, each the complementary counterpart of the other. Only when the two sexes, masculine and feminine, are united does sexual relation signify completion or communion. Sexual love therefore must be heterosexual. Homosexual love is intrinsically narcissistic or incomplete. The homosexual loves only himself (herself) in reflection and not the "other." Eugene Bianchi, especially in his essay on "The Super-Bowl Culture of Male Violence," has described the fears of effeminacy that are typical of a masculinist society and the way in which the rejection of homosexuality is related to the repression of the gentle side of men.

Such a concept of complementarity depends on a sadomasochistic concept of male and female relations. It covertly demands the continued dependency and underdevelopment of woman in order to validate the thesis that two kinds of personalities exist by nature in males and females and which are each partial expressions of some larger whole. Such a view can allow neither men nor women to be whole persons who can develop both their active and their affective sides. Once women reject this psychology of dependency and that repression of their active and intellectual traits that is implied by the ideology of femininity, the myth of complementarity is overthrown. This concept of complementarity must be recognized as a false biologism that attempts to totalize on the level of the whole human existence a limited functional complementarity that exists on the level of procreative systems. Procreative systems—vagina and penis, sperm and ovum—might seem like two opposite sides of a process that only together become a whole, a new person. But even complementarity on this level has traditionally created false myths about women by denying that women had an ovum that was equally a seed to the male sperm (Aristotle) and attempting to repress the active orgasmic drive of women located in the clitoris (Freud and his ancestors back to primitive times).

When sex ceases to be limited to this procreative function and becomes a total bodily possibility of two persons this notion of opposites necessary to make a whole disappears. On the level of total organisms men and women both equally have all the organs of thinking, feeling and relating. It is meaningless to say that men are more active and women more receptive. The maintenance of this false biological analogy on the level of total psychophysical organisms depends on an elaborate conditioning of women to passivity and males to aggressiveness. The mind and the five senses are the organs of thinking and feeling in total organic existence, not penises and vaginas. Men and women are equally well-equipped with the psychophysical organs of thinking and feeling, action and receptivity. Only a distorted psychic conditioning of the two sexes into opposite personalities, formed by power relations of domination and subjugation, make them appear to be psychic opposites of each other, analogous to the superficial contraries of genitals.

Once sex is no longer confined to procreative genital acts and masculinity and femininity are exposed as social ideologies, then it is no longer possible to argue that sex/love between two persons of the same sex cannot be a valid embrace of bodily selves expressing love. If sex/love is centered primarily on communion between two persons rather than on biologistic concepts of procreative complementarity, then the love of two persons of the same sex need be no less than that of two persons of the opposite sex. Nor need their experience of ecstatic bodily communion be less valuable.

Both the woman's movement and the gay movement are moving

from the psychology of complementarity to the psychology of androgyny. Although the term itself retains all too clearly its dualistic origins, what it means is that both males and females contain the total human psychic essence. Men are just as capable of being receptive and intuitive as women; women are just as capable of being thinkers and decisive actors as men. Such a view of persons as androgynous is not antibiological as some have claimed. It is a correction to the false biology presupposed by the doctrine of complementarity. It is a simple recognition that people hear with their ears, feel with their bodies and think with their brains. People don't hear with their vaginas and think with their penises. Men and women equally have the organs of psychic activity and receptivity. Psychically men and women are not complementary but "mutual."

Authentic mutuality means not only that men speak and women hear, but that women also speak and men hear. It means that men and women cease to be half personalities. Both must grow to unite the many sides of themselves through multiple relationships with other people. The strong active side of one can be complementary to the receptive side of another, but the receptive side can be nurtured by the emotive, receptive side of another in a way that is equally important for full human development. Head can nurture head, and heart can nurture heart. Men can nurture women in both intellectuality and aggressiveness and also in emotionality and receptiveness. And women can do the same for men. In still different ways men can nurture and challenge each other, and women can nurture and challenge each other. In androgynously developed persons it is not possible to rule out sex/love relations between women or between men. This also means that heterosexual and homosexual relations cease to be ideological contraries. Straight and gay can cease to occupy different worlds, the heterosexual world dominating the legitimate universe and the gay subculture lurking in the shadows. The politicization of the demand that a person be exclusively heterosexual or exclusively homosexual can be surpassed. Each person seeks his or her full soul by nurturing human wholeness in a plural (but not infinite) community of persons. Relations center upon personal respect and mutual development.

The unification of sexuality and in-depth interpersonal communication and commitment cannot be determined either by law or by gimmicks of instant encounter. Neither the legalistic approach that demands that two persons, once having been officially yoked, stick it out to the death even when their relationship has become primarily one of mutual destruction, nor that narcissistic promiscuity that would have us hopping endlessly from bed to bed corresponds to authentic intimacy. There is a need for covenants of commitment for better or for worse as long as even the "for worse" belongs to a growth relationship. But such commitments cannot rule out other sex/love friendships entirely even if our present proprietary traditions of sexuality make it very difficult to develop such plurality in a mature way, without elements of jealousy and hurt. There may also be a need for the techniques of the encounter movement that help to break down our body alienation and open us up to our untapped potential for total psychophysical ecstasy and self-disclosure. But instant turn-on's are not committed friendships.

Real intimacy must be a profound creation. Its guides are those of personal friendship and commitment to mutual growth. This cannot be done by a technological concept of psychic or sexual functions. Nor can it be tied to exclusivistic marriages when friendship is irreparably blocked or when sexuality and subsistence are exchanged only on superficial or bruta-lized levels. Intimacy is a creative activity whereby over some period of time of sharing, growth and exploration we find ways to open ourselves to the beloved other person on deepening levels. We learn slowly to create our body-selves as the sacrament of personal communication, restoring to our sexuality that power of grace that we usually relegate to a docetic spirituality. This takes place only between people who share their deepest selves, who risk bad moments as well as good ones with each other. It takes place between people who are seeking truthfulness, who are engaged in a project of mutual growth, who can support each other's development even in directions that may take a part of the person away into other communities of work and relationship. This is hardly possible when woman is domesticated and man's work goes on in a sphere alienated from "woman's place." It is possible only when women are freed from underdevelopment and dependency and men from a false self-sufficiency. It is possible only when people are colleagues as well as lovers who share life and work in a quest to give birth to each other's fullest selves. This is the mystery that has been pointed out and promised when we speak of love. But it is a threatening and morally exacting task that we usually avoid and deny in our sexist and atrophied marriages, our hasty sexuality and our narcissistic demand for instant intimacy.

Notes: Chapter V

1. Sigmund Freud, *Collected Papers.* London: Hogarth Press, 1950, vol. IV, pp. 203-17.

2. William Morris, "The Society of the Future," cited in Sheila Rowbotham, *Women, Resistence and Revolution: A History of Women and Revolution in the Western World.* New York: Vintage, 1974, p. 89.

3. Hans Jonas, *The Gnostic Religion: The Message of the Alien God and the Beginnings of Christianity.* Boston: Beacon, 1958, pp. 270-7. J. B. Russell, *Witchcraft in the Middle Ages.* Cornell University Press, 1972, pp. 127ff.

4. The allegorical interpretation of the "Song of Songs" as the love between Israel and Yahweh had been established in rabbinic commentary by the first century A.D. Origen's "Commentary on the Song of Songs" established the Christian mystical use of it as the sacred marriage between the soul and Christ. This interpretation was the basis for its use as the primary text for contemplative theology in the Middle Ages, as in the commentaries by Bernard of Clairvaux, William of St. Thierry and many others.

5. "Lenin on the Woman Question," by Clara Zetkin, from *The Emancipation of Women,* writings of V. I. Lenin. New York: International Publishers, 1934, Appendix, pp. 95-123.

6. William Reich, *Sex-Pol Essays, 1929-34.* Ed. Lee Baxandall. Intro., Bertell Ollmann. New York: Vintage Press, 1972.

7. Raymond Lawrence, "Toward a More Flexible Monogamy," *Christianity and Crisis,* 34/4 (March 18, 1974), pp. 42-47.

Chapter VI

Psychic Celibacy and the Quest for Mutuality

Eugene C. Bianchi

After spending twenty years of my life in the Jesuit Order of the Catholic Church, I thought I knew something about celibacy, but I found out how confined and inadequate my notion of celibacy was when I resigned from the clergy and experienced marriage and sex in our culture. For a long time I thought that celibacy was a prerogative unique to the Catholic clergy and nuns. Now I realize that celibacy is deeply rooted in our society at large.

Does this sound preposterous in the age of Hugh Hefner, the pill and permissiveness? Maybe it will help if I distinguish between physical and psychic celibacy. The physical celibate renounces sexual contact with the opposite sex or with another of one's own sex. Rules for Catholic religious professionals still insist on this kind of celibacy, although the post-Vatican Council II environment threatens old restrictions. Psychic celibacy consists in keeping women mentally and affectionally at arm's length. It is in fact the core dogma of our patriarchal era. Woman can be exalted as wife, virgin, mother, or deprecated (and enjoyed) as temptress, playmate, whore. In whatever way this male projection works woman is object, nonequal, manipulated, distanced. Such a world is profoundly celibate.

The Church has certainly made a major contribution to psychic celibacy in Western culture. Centuries of physical celibacy for priests and nuns succeeded in excluding the feminine factor from higher ecclesiastical decision-making. The rejection of physical sexuality tended to corroborate the distancing of woman from the zone of intellect and spirituality. Physical celibacy has also harmed affectional growth for many Church professionals, although some have developed warm and loving personalities without sexual relations. Yet, even in Church circles, where traditional celibacy has been abandoned, the psychic mode prevails. The higher up the ladder one goes in Protestant hierarchies the scarcer women become. Deliberation and decision at the top take place in a male lodge where the cultural myths of masculinity reign supreme.

From earliest times churchmen have not regarded woman as a full person and equal companion. Christianity began in a culture pervaded by dualistic male projection: body and woman means bad; mind and man means good. Wherever two or three (read men) were gathered together, the Gospel tells us, God and Church were present. Reread the ninth and tenth commandments about coveting a neighbor's wife and property. Woman, classified among things, was not a fit subject for friendship that called for equality of human condition. In Paul's perspective, woman was mainly an impediment to mission, except perhaps for certain of her ancillary functions. In cultivating its psychic celibacy Christianity said a resounding "no" to homosexual affection, and it proclaimed an equally loud "no" to women as anything more than animate possessions.

This condition of psychic celibacy mirrored in the Church is magnified in every dimension of our society. Boys are reared to join associations of males that in both fact and intent exclude females. The principal orientation of masculine identity is toward competition and success in a world of men. At their points of wide-ranging influence, government, business and the professions are ruled by nearly all-male groups. Watergate provides a perfect example of the masculine-only phenomena in the highest reaches of state. When a woman finally appears in the long line of conspirators she is a secretary who fails to properly operate a tape recorder. Big-time football manifests in cultural microcosm the celibate domain where men compete with rationalized brutality for gain and status. Self-valuation as a man person depends on how well he performs against other men.

Woman's place is one of enforced psychic celibacy. She is not encountered as a contributing equal to men in occupational and civic life. When she is admitted to the executive and professional planes she needs to prove her rationality at every step against the ingrained prejudices about female instability among her male colleagues. On the level of mind and decision in the public sphere there is little or no intercourse between men and women. In this realm our performance and profit society is as celibate as a Trappist monastery. Unwritten but very real "Cloister" signs hang outside the board rooms, menacing excommunication (subtle and crass discriminations) for trespassing.

I would have expected a relaxation of psychic celibacy in domestic and recreational activities. But even here woman's role is ancillary and compensatory; it is usually not one of mutual exchange among equally sharing persons. As wife and mother she tends the hearth to free men to build their egos in a community of male peers. Women as wives, daughters, sisters, lovers are the working nuns of America; they clear a way and a time for their high priests to attend to sacred priorities. The woman widowed by weekend TV football is a symptom of the psychic celibacy syndrome. That many women refuse to recognize their situation is not surprising. Having internalized the system, they find derivative self-worth by imitation of the master class and enjoyment of material pacifiers.

When men turn to women for sexual relief from the tensions of the job grind it is often done as an act with a subordinate rather than as a relationship with a cherished equal. Cheerleaders, bunnies and broads of all varieties are strictly sideline diversions to help the boys return refreshed to the all-male playing field. Physical sex in our culture is performed in an atmosphere of psychic celibacy. Sex needs to be compartmentalized and controlled in the male mentality lest its offshoots of tenderness and warm concern distract them from making it in the competitive arena of peers. A growing number of women are giving up on men as partners for loving relationships beyond the sex act.

Two presuppositions underlie this vision of a psychically celibate country. First, it is harmful all around, and, second, women at this stage in history have developed virtues that are desperately needed to counterbalance qualities drummed into males. Survival of the species will depend on a new interplay of masculine and feminine perspectives. That the regnant world of the male club is destructive needs little proof. When unchecked, the tough qualities of aggressive competition and manipulative technological rationality lead to Theodore Roszak's "wargasm" at home and abroad. The culminating image of contemporary maleness is the Pentagon, America's model monastery on the Potomac. There the crusaders are ever poised for the next holy war.

To my mind it is fruitless to argue whether the best of feminine qualities stem from nature or from nurture. Whether natural or the result of socialization (the probable answer) the traits of compassion, intuition, cooperation, unifying acceptance of nature and people have been far more cultivated among women. This feminine dimension is latent but stunted in most men, especially among those who rise to commanding positions in a milieu where toughness is paramount. Our national environment of psychic celibacy stimulates the personal and social destructiveness of these unbalanced proclivities.

There is no facile formula for developing a more harmonious blend of what have been called traditionally masculine and feminine qualities in each of us. Yet our long patriarchy-dominated history reveals numerous attempts to envision and enact androgynous human interaction. I understand the concept of androgyny in this context as the individual and social possibility for fostering in men and women qualities that have conventionally been restricted to one of the sexes. Androgyny, or mutuality, also implies the corollary of lessening the exaggerated and harmful development of masculine and feminine virtues. An example from classical Greek society of the impulse toward androgyny was the presence of *hetairae*. These were gracefully educated women who had influence in the public sphere through their qualities of wit and intuition. Such women were free of household tasks and child-rearing to be able to involve themselves in the civilizing pursuits of literature, poetry, dance and philosophy. The leaders of this basically male-dominated society understood the social need for feminine presence beyond the private realm of the household. I am not looking to the Athenian situation as an ideal to be restored as it originally existed. That context was still sexist; I am pointing only to the societal recognition of androgynous benefits. Hellenic sages, mostly men, admitted the vital contribution to a more complete culture made by the *hetairae*.

In the medieval Church an excessively male hierarchy with its masculine theology was somewhat balanced by the exalted place of the Virgin Mary. Although I have negatively criticized Marian devotion in another essay, the positive influence of the Virgin also merits attention. The traits of nurturing, gentleness and receptivity were preserved in the cults of Mary and other women saints. Without a valid sense of female personhood in everyday life, the clerical celibate culture of the Middle Ages tended to distort these virtues by assigning them to an ethereal feminine sphere. Though the gentle emotions and intuitions had some residual impact, medieval men saw these qualities as inferior to male attributes,. Moreover, these feminine virtues were thought of as potentially destructive of virility if they were cultivated by men. Such an attitude remains common in American society. Toys, dress, activities and expectations are still rigidly separated for boys and girls. In our society, grounded on the tough qualities of competition for status and self-worth, the feminine virtues are confined to the private sphere of the family. In the public arena these qualities threaten to undermine political and economic power-dominance. The "soft" virtues also raise the fear of homosexuality, especially among men whose self-identity depends so vitally on the rugged qualities of masculinity.

An androgynous culture or a society of mutuality would not be based on traits defined according to gender. Social roles and personal behavior would be freely chosen by men and women without legal and informal pressure to conform to stereotypical patterns. The renewed interest of recent years in tribal and traditional cultures has disclosed some noteworthy tendencies toward androgyny. These "primitive" societies often achieved an androgynous balance in more integrated ways than did the major dominant civilizations of East and West. Symbol, myth and ritual in tribal society acknowledged the primal power of the feminine, although this force was also feared by males. In African and other cultures, for example, the symbol of the serpent swallowing its own tail signified not only the infinite and immortal but also the integration of male and female. Most traditional cultures, whether nomadic or agricultural, had a deep appreciation and awe for the feminine dimensions of divinity. These peoples conserved a sense of being part of nature as reflective extensions of the creativity and fertility of Mother Earth. With the advance of rational learning and technology, the feminine principle as matrix of all creatures has been alienated from the zone of male mind and activity. The ecological neglect and perversion of our time is related to the subordination of feminine sensitivity toward nature. The objectifying male mind tends to render impersonal and detached from the self all other beings. Modern men do not see themselves as continuations of earth or as rhythmically and essentially part of a wider natural support system. Western religious dichotomies between history and nature, heavenly grace and earthly existence have only aggravated the masculine propensity to alienate men from feminine sensitivities.

The intense estrangement of male from female, and the pervasive subordination of the latter in our heritage, have made the restoration of an androgynous balance very difficult. In the medieval *roman* the theme of courtly love emphasized the attractiveness of the feminine. But this attempt to redress the balance failed in terms of healthy androgyny because the female qualities were both overly romanticized and unincorporated by men. Troubadours could sing of fair maidens, and knights would perform exploits for them. Yet women were confinded to fixed and inferior roles in society; for the most part they had no opportunities to exercise their talents in the public realm. Another example of the skewed attempt to achieve an equalibrium of mutuality between the sexes can be sighted in the characterizations of heroic women in the works of Ariosto and Spenser. The fictional genius of these writers enveloped special women with epic and Amazonian properties. But just as the ideal of romantic love distorted the balance of androgyny on the side of womanly tenderness, so too the portrayal of conquering heroines served mainly to transfer male warrior qualities to women. The exaggeration of the heroic female becomes a captivating fantasy for the literary imagination, but it does not depict realizable attributes in the actual culture. Translated into contemporary terms, the propensity to create the Amazonian ideal for women is akin to encouraging them to enter the male world of work with the same violence-prone ethos of competition cultivated by men.

Glimpses and elaborations of a constructive and feasible androgyny had to await the 19th and early 20th centuries. A number of historical factors conspired to foster this development. As Rosemary Ruether explains (cf. Chapter III), woman's plight in industrialized Victorian society reduced her to a privatized, morality fixture for the solace and aid of men. The movement from agrarian to urban society sealed women in rigid patterns of given feminine traits according to their class in the culture. The Victorian lady and the lower-class mill girl were oppressed in different ways, but both experienced severe limitations of choice in cultivating personal attributes and social roles. Yet in this same 19th century context—the first great wave of the women's movement—reaction against the repressive situation unleashed realistic possibilities for an androgynous social order. By a curious turn of history, technological society, dominated by the male psyche with its limited and inadequate qualities of virility, made possible a women's movement that could efficiently challenge those exclusively male attributes and perquisites. Technology gradually freed women from the unrelenting demands of household tasks and child-rearing. Industrialized urban life did not call for the large families that kept women tied to prescribed roles. More importantly, technological society with its underlying democratic leanings needed a broadly educated population to occupy technical and managerial positions. Educational institutions began to open up to women. Although this training was directed mainly to cultivating more interesting subordinates for men and better tutors for their children, it also helped a significant number of women to lead a movement for justice and new options. This women's movement from the 1848 declaration at Seneca Falls, New York, to the attainment of suffrage after World War I, spearheaded the drive for equality and opportunity—prerequisites for an androgynous culture.

In the historical context of the last century and a half major writers began to deal with the realistic prospects for a culture of mutuality. Their style was frequently one of confrontation with regnant social values, but its direction was clear. The ideals of the feminist movement were far from being realized, but at least they were perceived as possible and necessary. John Stuart Mill spoke out strongly against the structures of discrimination that impeded a society of mutuality. Engels reminded his followers that a criterion of a civilization's advancement was the status of its women. Ibsen not only classically depicted the modern struggle for women's options in Nora of *A Doll's House*, he also stated the crucial problem of his social milieu, an order controlled by a restricted set of masculine traits: "Your society is a society of bachelor souls" (*Pillars of Society*). Shaw's *St. Joan* dramatized with unprecedented power the attainment in a single person of the qualities of strength, courage, compassion and sensitivity. Virginia Woolf and the Bloomsbury group expressed a novel mixture of male and female attributes both in literary works and in their life styles. It is important to place ourselves in the framework of this history if we would appreciate the prospect of yet unrealized male/female interactions. Recognizing the advances and restrictions of our contemporary scene, we can start to shape a realistic education toward the development of androgynous men and women. In this way we can avoid the disastrous consequences of psychic celibacy.

The path from psychic celibacy to a male/female mutuality in our society needs to be carefully explored and followed. In her discussion of homosexuality (cf. Chapter V, "The Personalization of Sexuality"), Ruether points out the biological bias by which we ascribe psychic human traits to one sex and not to the other. I agree with her assessment of the error in this rigid duality of characteristics as it has been traditionally applied to the condemnation of homosexuality for its "unnaturalness."

But we also need to examine closely the conventional usage of male and female traits in the heterosexual context. Is it possible and desirable for men and women to cultivate qualities that have historically been assigned to the opposite sex? What would be the consequences for individuals and for society of such a mutation of attitudes and behaviors? It will be no easy task in any event to change ideas and feelings about what is given as male and female. Such alterations in personal and social expectations threaten a long-established sense of virility among men. Moreover, such an upheaval would appear to undermine the privileged positions that have traditionally been held by men. Fear of changing old traits may be even stronger among women, who in general experience insecurity concerning finances and status. Afraid to lose the flimsy props of femininity that give them a modicum of security in a man's world, these women become the staunchest enemies of "women's lib." Because of these anxieties they often betray and satirize other women who try to cultivate so-called masculine qualities and who pursue male-type careers.

These fears and insecurities among men and women are the greatest obstacles to overcoming the harmful polarization of roles and traits. Yet beneath the anxieties about losing what self-worth the conventional characteristics afford us lurks the impulse toward wholeness implied in androgyny. Our fears on this subject will be partially allayed by risking to educate children in an atmosphere of sexual mutuality rather than one of strict complementarity. In the former way, any conventional male or female trait can be developed by either sex depending only on one's talents and choices. The latter form of education divides styles of behavior according to gender and looks to a complementarity of strictly female and male traits. In the family, children should be able to witness rationality and emotion, assertiveness and receptivity, public and private roles in adults of both sexes. If parents are aware of the alienating sexual dualisms in the culture and if they are attentive to their own promptings toward wholeness they will want to expose all children to the whole gamut of human experiences. Parents and teachers will correct sex-role stereotyping in formal education. Text books, field projects, recreational activity and counseling for children need to be recast. Girls especially should be encouraged to develop strong bodies and many forms of physical dexterity presently reserved for boys. A key, though overlooked, factor in the subordination of women is an education for physical insecurity and excessive bodily dependence. Another vital need in an education for mutuality is the fostering of studies that stimulate the contemplative, mythic, poetic and intuitive aspects of life. This topic implies a wholesale revamping of curriculum and methods of teaching, a subject beyond the scope of this essay. But meditative and affectional education is especially necessary as a counterbalance to the intense orientation of our schools towards competitive vocationalism. The rational and utilitarian is being exclusively cultivated at the expense of essential humanizing needs in our students.

Yet the difficulty of accomplishing these goals becomes evident when we consider the conflicting messages that children and adults receive in America. While family and school might be making progress in educating for androgyny, the media and the peer group often influence us to conform to sex-role conventions. For the sake of financial success, television and cinema depend to a large extent on perpetuating prejudices. Media and entertainment industries are themselves controlled by the national and international economic and political reward system, which is deeply entrenched in sex-role polarization. Political officials, corporation executives, leading professionals are almost all males. Conditioned in an environment of sexism, these men would judge an adrogynous education as a threat to personal power and an order of reality that is now beneficial to them. Indicative of this situation is the stubborn reluctance of professional and collegiate athletics to promote the full-scale participation of women in sports. This attitude is approaching the controversial level in colleges where antisexual discrimination legislation challenges a disproportionate use of funds for male athletic endeavors. Another example of the defensiveness of patriarchy in holding on to its privileges is the inability of Hollywood to deal with the new consciousness of many women. Commentators have noted the absence of top female stars by comparison with the Thirties and Forties. Yet the film industry continues for the most part to present women on screen as tragic but subordinate creatures or as non-decision-making sexpots. The cinema czars thus ignore the talent potential of the new woman (and of the androgynous man), propagate harmful sexrole stereotyping and make an androgynous culture more difficult to achieve.

This issue of new options for women in a society of mutuality confronts men with a significant question on a personal and social level: Is it beneficial for males to defend and promote the structures and ideologies of psychic celibacy? If we begin with the premise that conventional masculine and feminine qualities are potentially present in men as well as in women the exclusive development of one set of these traits is a perversion of human growth. We have few models in a sexist society of androgynous men and women. Yet it can be shown that some of the most creative people in arts and sciences manifest an unusual mixture of masculine and feminine aspects in their personalities. While these unique individuals can point the way to a culture of mutuality, the strongest argument in support of androgyny arises from an examination of the results in our society of the presently ruling images of *machismo* and of the feminine ideal. I have previously dealt with negative consequences for men and for society as a whole stemming from the sexist formation of the male psyche. At this point it would be good to review some of the positive advantages to both men and women in the cultivation of virtues ordinarily ascribed to the opposite sex.

If women learn to be more straightforwardly assertive (I prefer "assertive" to "aggressive" because of the connotations of violence in the latter) they would have less occasion to suffer from unhealthy repression and displacement of real needs and legitimate ambitions. Direct feminine assertiveness would teach the wider society that women can lead and originate as well as be led and be imitative. Men could relax from the incessant demands of patriarchal culture to prove themselves worthy by making, controlling and achieving. If we men tempered in ourselves the deeply indulcated drive to compete for the self-meaning that wealth and power falsely promise we would be better able to develop in ourselves the qualities of inner calm and enriching receptivity. It may appear strange in a culture of action-oriented males to advocate the passive virtues of silent listening and humble receptivity. Yet I believe that many men suppress the mystic and poetic dimensions of their personalities, realms that could bring them great satisfaction and growth in humanity. It is encouraging to note that an increasing number of men are now involved in various forms of meditation as well as in charismatic and other spiritual movements. A balancing of feminine assertiveness and male receptivity would help both sexes move toward personal wholeness; this equilibrium would also have important social benefits by mitigating the exaggerations in male and female development that contribute to hostility and violence.

The feminist movement has rightly supported a new spirit of independence among women. The strength to be self-sufficient and to be in touch with their own inner power is a necessary corrective to the culturally-induced traits of dependence and submissiveness. While this attitude of independence will increase her options, it also requires a certain financial independence for women. Such personal and occupational independence will diminish the regrets, self-recriminations and resentments that a large number of middle-aged women feel for having permitted themselves to be derivative and ancillary adjuncts to male careers. Moreover, a vast amount of womanly talent in all fields has been denied by the submissive roles forced on women for centuries. While excessive dependence is harmful to both sexes, men could benefit from opening themselves to a certain kind of dependence. This means a dependence that recognizes one's own limitations and one's corresponding need to accept help from others. It is a wonderful quality to know how to receive graciously from others in the understanding that we are by nature receptive as well as giving creatures. In learning how to receive, to welcome the gifts or the gift of the other, we make possible the dialogue of friendship. Friendship calls for giving and receiving, sharing and taking. Receptive dependence is also intimately linked to the religious act of faith in which the divine first gives itself to humans in spiritual experience. In sum, men cut themselves off from full religious growth by their excessive independence.

Watching the two congresswomen on the House Judiciary Committee during the impeachment debate brought home to many observers the rational clarity and the power of conviction of which women are capable. It is important to mark and multiply these happenings as a counterbalance to the popular prejudice of exaggerated female emotionality. Women have been victimized in patriarchal culture by the propagation of the untruth that they by nature concentrate on the emotionally personal and not on the universal and intellectual. The nurturing role of woman has no doubt fostered valuable qualities of personal concern, empathy and compassion. But the stereotype of nonrational woman needs to be attacked wherever it appears. We men by contrast have been taught to deny our emotions in a vain and truncated pursuit of rationality. Men's liberation groups today are keenly aware of this lack in our formation. To express emotion, especially the "soft" emotions associated with tears or tenderness, is judged to be a sign of weakness in males.

Yet the result of this influential stereotype has been the blocking of deeper friendships among men. Their conversation is usually restricted to politics, business and sports. Rarely do they admit to feelings of elation, wonder, fear or sadness. Without the ability to express these emotions, men preserve a sham, defensive veneer over their vulnerabilities. It is understandable that men want to avoid being hurt by appearing vulnerable. But they also deprive themselves by their defensiveness of going beneath the surface of business and golf-acquaintance relations with other men to embrace and sustain each other at deeper levels. The lack of affectional development in men also impairs their ability to improve relationships with women. One of the most universal complaints of women, especially in marriages of some duration, is the dearth of personal interest and emotional support shown by their men. This situation is exacerbated by the confinement of female roles and by the pressures on men to achieve in occupational pursuits. But external factors alone do not account for lack of affectional response in men. We have not placed emotional sensitivity high on our priority list; it is even a suspect value among us men. This is unfortunate because it stunts friendship with the women closest to us and with our potential male friends. Because friendship is among the greatest gifts of life, its androgynous roots need cultivating.

Another popularly accepted division of qualities is that of submissiveness and weakness for females and aggressiveness and strength for males. Our present world of psychic celibacy is so thoroughly steeped in such a duality that it is unconsciously assimilated as a fixed law of nature. Because this masculine projection about the docility and fragility of women is so basic to all sexist structures it becomes especially important for women to challenge this governing axiom of patriarchy. As more women become aware of this anti-feminist myth they will want to develop both physical strength and the ability to clearly and forthrightly assert their needs and desires. It is, of course, easier to write or say this than to realize it in the face of social pressures to the contrary. Strong and self-assertive women risk being classified as nonfeminine, as destroyers of men. Yet more women are engaging in physical activities that in the past were considered too strenuous for them. They are also entering occupations and professions that were previously the domain of men only. We can hope that in all these involvements women will both activate their new-found potential and bring to leisure and work their traditional gifts of empathy and compassion.

Because women are more conscious of sexism than men, endeavors to balance the virtues of assertion and listening, of strength and other-oriented sensitivity in the female personality will have a most significant influence on men. The initial male reaction may be surprised repulsion or subtly mocking humor, but the educational effect of such women will eventually be enormous both on male children and adults. It will gradually alter the warrior syndrome by which men judge their own worth and that of their fellows in the various male lodges directing our society. The single most destructive dimension of being a man is the long indoctrination in this warrior syndrome of aggressiveness, as I have argued in my essay on the male mystique of violence. Whether on the playing field, in the board room or on the battlefield men feel that they must be aggressive and dominant to succeed. In the male club, healthy aspects of assertiveness become pathogenic because they are exaggerated into distortions. The result is a kind of generalized militarism, a passion to conquer others in sport, business, government and other fields. The other man is always the enemy who may steal away my status, power and self-esteem. He must be kept in his place—made subservient to my dictates, made "woman"—or soundly defeated and thus taught a fearsome lesson. In such a milieu, an ethic of justice and compassion is impossible; the country is no longer ruled by law but by the power ambitions of men.

My hope for a society of mutuality depends largely on aware and daring women who will enter into all the strongholds of male militarism. The educational consequence of this movement will be to give women confidence about their abilities to operate well at all decision-making levels. It will also provide new models for younger women who seek outlets for their talents. Such opportunities and activities will also mitigate some of the depression and resentment that women experience in a culture that sharply limits their human potential. In *Women and Madness*, Phyllis Chesler graphically describes the social conditioning that induces mental disturbances in women. Her concluding prescription for a healthy female psyche is congruent with my theme about fostering polar attitudes and actions:

> Woman's ego-identity must somehow shift and be moored upon what is necessary for her own survival as a strong individual. Women must somehow free themselves to be concerned with many things and ideas, and with many people. Such a radical shift in ego-focus is extremely difficult and very frightening. It grates and screeches against the grain of all "feminine" nerves and feelings, and implies grave retribution.

This shift in ego-identity, however cannot be accomplished without active involvement in spheres that were once thought of as unfeminine. Support from other women and from sympathetic men is important, but ultimately the new woman must be self-activating if her liberating understanding is not to remain academic.

The influence of these liberated women on men will also be positive on both personal and social levels. Men will come to see that their human value does not depend on achievements as tribal warriors. Males will discover that they can be assertive without the compulsion to dominate enemies, an inclination born of their own insecurities about self-esteem. One's competitor may win or lose and still be a friend. The concrete result of the transaction will not be the determinant of the worth of either man. With this possibility of deeper male friendship (and of male/female friendships, not merely sexual contacts), an androgenous, anti-militaristic culture can evolve. The benefits for men and for all peoples on the social plane would be great.

In making this claim I do not expect a utopia without tears and pain; the word utopia means "not-a-place." I realize only too well that we live in very finite definite places, *topoi* of finitude and unavoidable brokenness. But a gradual evolution of the male psyche away from the warrior syndrome of self-understanding would significantly affect the grave challenges to national and world welfare. The problems of world food shortages and overpopulation, of nuclear weapons and ecological deterioration will not disappear. But all these issues are immensely aggravated by men who deal with them under the dictates of the warrior syndrome. How can it be otherwise if the world and its peoples are conceived of as enemies to this individual and to his power clique in the male lodge? The promise of the women's movement as it affects men could be a profound shift in attitude towards caring about the world in a serving and nurturing way. The feminine quality of nurturing children could be transformed into nurturing the earth and its children. Such a humanistic attitude would cast a novel perspective on the pressing macro-problems before us.

These benefits of an androgenous civilization, however, depend upon deeper personal changes in all of us, both men and women. The growth towards a culture of mutuality has been described in the context of blending the better male and female qualities. Beneath this important process of changing characteristics is the root issue of accepting and loving our real selves. As long as we cling to masks and identify with them, the pivot point for re-educating ourselves as men and women will be missing. Unless we can begin to uncover the Archimedean position of self-loving self-acceptance, we anxiously and rigidly lock on to the disguise of given roles and traits. In this confinement we are unable to reach out to the other in a creative way because we do not know our own identity or the authenticity of the one doing the reaching. We confuse ourselves with our masks to protect the small and estranging comfort they offer. Although there is no single road to self-acceptance, an environment of sustaining and encouraging community is an essential element in this growth. The building of life-support communities of men and women, a subject beyond the scope of this essay, is crucial to the realization of its vision.

This matter of self-acceptance and other-acceptance is also intimately associated with the religious question of conversion and salvation. The turning away from the sham self and the ability to accept our true self have been spoken of in many religious heritages as the grace of conversion. This turning is never accomplished without some pain and doubt and risk; moreover, it is a continuing process in our lives. Yet this conversion to God is not something done primarily in a ritual service or in special religious language. It happens primordially in the warp and woof of the personal and social fabric of daily existence. This is why it is religiously important to examine and rectify the oppressive patterns by which we are formed as men and women. On the personal plane, our path toward wholeness demands first the recognition of our illness, the distorted qualities by which we become men and women. It also requires a willingness to explore new patterns of thinking and interaction in our own lives that will foster male/female reconciliation. In the social realm, America as militant monastery needs to reflect on a spiritual-psychic transformation as its second centenary approaches. Unless the nation's third century becomes more androgynous at every point, our soul-celibate chieftains will lead us to Armaggedon.

Chapter VII

Sexism and the Liberation of Women

Rosemary Ruether

"Women will be saved through bearing children" (I Tim. 2:15). In this crisp sentence the author of the Pastoral Epistles sums up what has been a normative view of woman's way to salvation in Christian history. A different view is offered by the Gnostic Gospel of the Egyptians (Clem. of Alex.; *Strom.* III:9,63): Here Jesus announces that "I have come to destroy the works of the female." What is meant by this statement is that Jesus has come to destroy the works of sexual feeling and maternity. He has come to put an end to the making of babies. Only when the processes of becoming represented by procreation are brought to an end can the cycle of entrapment in the fallen cosmos be overcome and the spirit return to its true home in heaven. Women then are saved by "becoming male," by renouncing the maternal function and being transformed into the realm of disincarnate spirituality beyond sexuality.

"You are the Devil's gateway," cries Tertullian in a famous phrase from his *De Cultu Feminarum*, and he decrees for women a doubled repression, not only of their bodily feelings, but of their feminine image as well, as the price of the presumed "original" culpability of women for causing the fall of Adam.

These classic notions of the special burdens they are to accept as their place in the scheme of salvation must be analyzed by feminists as a part of the problem, not a part of the solution. Quite simply this means that the very analysis of sin or the fall, according to such male ideologies, must be recognized as being an expression of a fallen state of human relationships that finds its fundamental imagery in body alienation and sexual oppression. The scenarios of salvation dictated by this ideology cannot be salvific for women. On the contrary, they are simply restatements or recapitulations of the problem.

Much the same inversion appears in Freudianism, indicating to what extent psychoanalysis stands as the secular form of traditional religious sexism. The very analysis of woman's dilemma in Freud takes the classic form of dictating a way of salvation for women that is designed to recreate or reinforce the very neurosis by which women's "nature" is defined. Women for Freud are castrated beings, lacking by nature the male qualities of initiative and intellect. Lacking the capacity for intellectual and autonomous activity, women become neurotic or hysterical, according to Freud, when they engage in a wrongheaded effort to possess this autonomy, will and intellect that their lack of a penis must ever debar them from attaining. This desire is woman's sin. Salvation for women lies in giving up this "penis-envy" and resigning themselves to maternity and that passive, dependent relationship to men that is their anatomical destiny.[1] Again, as in I Timothy, we are told that women shall be saved by bearing children. The very road of autonomy and self-esteem that in the male would be regarded as mature and healthy is analyzed as sick-making. Women are directed down a road to health that would be regarded as the road to neurosis for the male. Only rarely do Freudians pause to wonder why 80 percent of the mental patients are women while 80 percent of the therapists are male. Even Freud at the end of his life cried out in puzzlement that he "didn't know what it was that women wanted." It is for these reasons that women have become so alienated from the male healers, whether they be doctors or priests. The male healers have revealed themselves as sick-makers. Women must overthrow these sick-making prescriptions of sin and salvation. They must begin to believe in themselves and their own experience and to sin bravely against the male formulas for salvation.

We must begin by understanding the nature of sexism as sin. If the fall consists in an alienation between man and God that takes social form in the alienated oppressive social relationship between persons, then sexism must be seen as the original and primary model for analyzing the state of the fall. This alienation begins in self-alienation, experienced as an alienation between the self and the body. The alienated oppressive relationship of man to woman is essentially a social projection of the self-alienation that translates certain initial biological advantages into a power relationship. This power relationship is totalized in social structures and modes of cultural formation that eliminate woman's autonomous personhood to define her solely in terms of male needs. In classical times this took the form of an identification of women with the lower half of self-alienated experience. Woman was stultifying matter opposing male intellectuality. Woman was emotionality and sexuality opposing male spirituality. Woman was the power of the past, the immanent, the static, opposing male mobility and transcendence. These images become self-fulfilling prophecies by socially incarnating and culturally enforcing them by excluding women from education and participation in public life and by immobilizing them in the home. By forbidding enlarging cultural experiences woman internalizes these images in herself. One shapes her to be what she symbolizes in the eye of self-alienated male perception. Women become the victims of that very process by which the male seeks to triumph over the conflict represented by these dualities. Women were limited and repressed into that very sphere of immanence and materiality the male sought to escape, transcend and dominate.

The fear of sexuality is the primary way of experiencing this self-alienation of mind from body. Women are depersonalized through this alienation and translated into a body-object to be used or abused sexually but not really encounterd through sexuality as a person. Male/female relations are envisioned as a kind of social extension of mind/body relations. This implies a subject/object or I/It relation between men and women sexually. This very way of envisioning the body as an alien object that wars against the soul corresponds to the subject/object relationship, reducing the other person to the status of a "thing" to be used. The characteristic of the subject/object relation between persons is that of the negation of the other as a "thou" to be met in and through the bodily presence. It also abolishes the possibility of bodily relations as the sacrament of mutuality and inter-subjectivity. In classical Christian spirituality the translation of male/female relations into an analogue of self-alienated body/mind dualism blotted out the possibility of bodily relations as a real meeting of persons. It constricted sexual relations into the framework of use or abuse. In the classical theories of sex, woman was defined as a sex object either rightly used for procreative or wrongly abused for carnal pleasure. In neither definition does woman appear as a person.

The ascetic and the libertine ways of depersonalizing woman as sex object are two sides of the same coin. We might call this the "Puritan-Prurient syndrome." Sex is either repressed and functionalized or sought after in a way that regards woman as a tool of male gratification. Either of these views, whether it uses woman for procreation, for relief of concupiscence or repudiates her as the image of debasing carnality must depersonalize her. The power relationship of supra- and subordination between men and women is essential to this schism. Only by making one person in the relation inferior, dependent and objectified as body, can one assure a sexuality without the demands of interpersonalism. By making woman a body one does not have to relate to her as a person. Asceticism is the nadir of patriarchalism in this respect. It does not have the effect of preventing the ascetic from having sexual experience, rather it assures that this experience will always be treated as sin, a debasing loss of control over the alien lower self that fantasizes women as the image of this debasing lower self, whether capitulated to or repudiated.

For those third-class citizens of the Church, the married, sex was permitted, but here too it was strictly functionalized within the ascetic definition of the "dirtiness" of sexual pleasure. Sexuality for the married was permitted only for procreation. But the erotic experience intrinsic in this act was regarded, especially in the Augustinian tradition, as sinful and indeed the vehicle for the transmission of original sin. This sin was forgiven the married if they despised the erotic experience itself and engaged in sex only for its good end in procreation, but sinfulness still adhered to the objective fact of orgasmic experience and was transmitted thereby to the child in the form of the taint of original sin. Dirty sex makes babies dirty and so the Blessed Event is not birth but baptism. By analyzing sex in this way one was prevented from recognizing that the real fall takes place in the dehumanization of woman. This is the real essence of that original sin that is not perpetuated through sex *biologically* but through *sexism*, morally and socially.

People are now seeking to throw off this heritage of sexual repression, but what is called the "sexual revolution" in the media often succeeds in doing little more than establishing the prurient side of this puritan schism. The sexual revolution began with Freud as a revolt against that hypocrisy of the Victorian family who repressed and sublimated sex in the home and compensated for this repression by the proliferation of houses of prostitution. There was a similar split in Southern society, with its repression and idealization of "virginal" white womanhood and its sexual exploitation of "carnal" black women. With the sexual revolution, women began to reclaim their rights to sexual experience. At first this was regarded as a profound threat to home and family, but it soon became apparent that the sexualizing of middle-class women could be as effective a way of tying them to traditional sexist relations as had been their earlier sexual repression. Indeed, this sexual revolution appeared at the very moment when the sexually repressive work culture of earlier capitalism was being transformed into the consumer society. The eroticization of the private sector of life was enlisted by the new consumer society both as the prime advertising image to sell consumer products and also as the chief means of pacifying the work alienation and political powerlessness of the male in public business. The split between home and work; the domesticated woman in the private sector and the alienated male sphere of business becomes all the more essential to the maintenance of consumer society. The domesticated female becomes the prime buyer of consumer products, just as her sexual image is used to whet the appetites of wasteful consumption. The home, which has lost all productive functions, is the voracious mouth devouring the products of consumer society. The domesticated woman is the chief tool of this process to whom the products of consumer society are sold through her own sexual image.

Even in the New Left, which was presumably in revolt against this bourgeois family, the sexist view of women was not criticized. Sexual liberation was understood in male terms simply as freedom to use women outside these confining structures. Radical women in the Sixties received a painful but galvanizing shock when they realized, in the words of Stokeley Carmichael, that the "only position for women in the Movement is prone." Women realized that they had been betrayed into a male-oriented sexual libertinism that was only the repressed side of puritanism but which had nothing to do with recognizing women as persons. The use of the word "fuck" in the counterculture, which makes the word for sexual intercourse interchangeable with expressions of disgust or dehumanizing exploitation, reveals the old schism. Making love continues to be a form of making war. In popular culture, sexual frankness begins to look more like pornography and becomes increasingly sadistic. In patriarchal cultures the repression and exploitation of women as both the despised and the desired body-object always appear as two sides of the same psychosocial alienation. In this context, the sexual revolution surfaces as the prurient side of puritan repression. It is not the liberation of women!

Sexual alienation and the depersonalizing of women defines the fall. But it cannot find salvation in its terms because its solutions only recapitulate the problem. Salvation can appear only as the resurrection of women, and the resurrection of woman means woman's self-definition as an autonomous person. She establishes herself as an autonomous person in any encounter rather than being co-oped into male projections that make her the image of male ideals or phobias. The resurrection of woman begins as an inner psychic revolution that gives her transcending power to disaffiliate herself from male objectifications, to depart from the incorporations of her as extensions of his demands and alienations.

We cannot underestimate the extent to which direct violence and the threat of physical violence has been a prime means of keeping women in a state of subserviency through the ages. This subjugation of women through the fear of male brutality has as its corollary the building up of males through sports and war to a confident aggressive use of their bodies and a parallel conditioning of women to meek, underdeveloped and unself-confident feelings about their own abilities to act or to defend themselves physically. Men of course have an advantage in biological musculature, although there are some women who are bigger and stronger than some men. But this advantage has been systematically cultivated to create a much greater polarization between male physical strength and female bodily helplessness than needs exist if women were trained in arts of selfdefense and built-up physically through sports. Traditional law codes, including that found in medieval Christian societies, sanctioned wife-beating as a proper punishment for resistence to the authority of males.[2] In many traditional societies, father or husbands even had the power of life or death over women. Wife-beating began to fade among middle-class Western Europeans in the 17th century, although it still survives in the lower classes even now. In Russia, China and Cuba the communist revolutions had to struggle to abolish this practice in the 20th century and to establish the wife as a person with a right to the integrity of her own person. In Russian peasant society it was common for the father-in-law to give the groom a new whip to be hung over the bed as a symbol of his authority. Large numbers of women were brutally murdered by their male relatives during the early years of the communist revolutions in these countries as the party endeavored to establish women's groups and to break the traditional patterns of female oppression.[3] There is no question that in many parts of the world, and even in large sectors of Western society, physical violence remains the last sanction that enforces male dominance.

Nevertheless, no oppression of a large group in society can be accomplished solely through open force. Oppression always seeks to become socially incorporated and to operate through modes of cultural conditioning that make the subjects internalize the image projected upon them and to accept it as their natural identity. Because, of all power relations, that between men and women is most intimate, it necessarily demands the most hidden forms of persuasion to shape women to become what they are supposed to be according to male ideology and to internalize this image as the one appropriate to their status. Women are culturally shaped from the earliest age to be the willing cooperators of their enslavement and to be unconscious of their objective situation.

Liberation begins as a terrifying explosion of consciousness for women, a self- and world-transcending conversion experience. Consciousness-raising parallels what blacks mean by black consciousness and what Latin Americans mean by *conscientization.* The theological virtues of liberation for the oppressed must be seen as the complementary opposites of the virtues of humbleness and gentleness that are necessary for the conversion from false power for the powerful. The sins of the oppressed are not pride and aggression but apathy and self-hatred. Hence it is necessary to preach the virtues of self-confidence, self-love and moral indignation to the oppressed. Anger corresponds to the power to transcend apathy and resignation and to break its chains, to no longer accepting evil systems of power as necessary or inevitable. Self-esteem corresponds to the exorcism of demeaning self-images and the re-establishment of an authentic sense of one's personhood in the image of God as the ground of one's being, out of which one has the confidence to struggle against the dehumanization of the self or others.

Superficially, this preaching of anger and self-esteem appears to negate the traditional Christian virtues. But the virtues of self-abnegation and humility are the correctives to the sins of the powerful, not the sins of the powerless. The mistake comes in confusing moral indignation and healthy self-love with that pride and hatred that exalts oneself by refusing community with others. That pride that is called "superbia," and its corollaries of hate and jealousy, absolutize the self at the expense of others. By contrast, moral indignation and self-esteem are rooted in community feeling. One is indignant at oppression because it denies the common humanity that underlies each person's self-affirmation. One affirms a humanity made in God's image not to negate others but to recover that common humanity that can unite us with others. Anger in the service of love and justice places all oppressive systems under judgment. For the oppressed, self-esteem resurrects the original and good nature underneath the distortions of self-hatred and demoralization wrought by denigration. Anger and self-esteem in this sense are theological virtues in the same way that faith and hope are theological virtues. They are the virtues that empower us to rise out of the present situation and set us on the way to a newly redeemed humanity. But they are not the final virtue of fulfillment. On the other side of the self-transcending wrath and reaffirmation of the humanity of the oppressed and the repentent conversion of the oppressors there remains love, the virtue of reconciliation and community. The ultimate theological virtue of love is not only eschatological, it is also primal. It represents the truth of community distorted by brokenness and sin. We could scarcely begin to struggle for it if we did not believe that this power of forgiveness and love was not already our authentic ground of being. Nevertheless, reconciliation cannot be used as cheap grace to enforce passivity and acceptance of status quo power systems. It can be taken for granted only by those who understand forgiveness, not as a mandate to do nothing, but as an empowerment to struggle against oppression and to remain restless and dissatisfied until "every tear is wiped away." Christians too often have used the preaching of forgiveness as a legitimization of present evil powers; forgiveness and reconciliation are preached as a pacification without the cross. The virtues of humility and meekness are preached not to the oppressors but to the oppressed, reenforcing their oppression. When Christian virtues are preached in this way they become a slave ethic, inculcating servility and enforcing acceptance of powers and principalities. Christianity becomes the religion of Caesar and ceases to be the Gospel of liberation.

For the oppressed, anger and self-esteem are transcendent and not expressions of the status quo. They represent the miraculous, the power of new being that breaks in from beyond their present condition, while at the same time restoring them to their true selves, the ground of their being. In this sense we can speak of the experience of anger and self-esteem for the oppressed as the presence and power of grace. Anger and self-esteem break the bonds of apathy and spring loose the trap of pacification and acceptance of evil. Anger and pride are the power for exodus, for disaffiliation from the bondage of male definition and use. This nay-saying is also a yea-saying, an ecstatic leap of consciousness, an élan of liberated power to be, transforming the basis of existence. Woman is empowered to depart from and define herself out of that subjugation to immanence of a male-centered transcendence that reduces the others to objects of domination. This exodus is a rebellion against the dead world of I/It relationships, reducing persons to things for exploitation and use by the sovereign ego of the master in whose image he made his God. It is the revelation of the possibility of cohumanity for the first time.

But this revelation of a new self and world remains proleptic and unfulfilled. It gives a foretaste of what a transformed humanity might look like. But the power structures of the fallen world remain even though their authority has been unmasked. Even when the legal subjugation that still defined the condition of women only a century ago has been largely repealed, economic and social ways of enforcing this subjugation remain. Women still find themselves encountered at every turn by falsifying role definition, sexist power plays and agonizing choices between equally debilitating alternatives. These are the typical conditions of life the male world offers women. Give up marriage and motherhood and we will let you compete in an inferior and handicapped way with ourselves, says the male world to women. If you don't care to be a celibate then be prepared to see the wasting of all your dreams for autonomous accomplishment. In somewhat modified form this is an updating of the old alternative between nun and married woman traditionally offered by the Church. A woman might rise to spirituality at the price of giving up marriage and sexuality or else accept the status of the married woman, to have no "head of her own" but to be under the dominion of her husband who is "her head."

These alternatives are not merely enforced by cultural conditioning. This ideology itself expresses the power relationships between men and women that are systemic to existing social and economic relationships. Socially, women from a caste within every class, meaning that they share a common oppression as women, but they find it hard to unite across class and racial lines because they are divided by the class and race oppression exercised by the ruling class and race over subjugated classes and races. As women they serve as the domestic servants of society, freeing the male for the work day by bearing all the auxiliary and supportive chores. When let into the work world they are generally structured into the same kind of domestic services and auxiliary support systems of male executive roles—as nurses, secretaries and the like. Economically, women provide the support system for male mobility and work. Domesticated in the private sector they are not only the auxiliary support system for male work and the child nurturers (for what has come in modern times to be an intensive and extended definition of childhood), but they also provide that sphere of rest, recreation and erotic life that pacifies male work alienation. Thus the cult of true womanhood, which seeks to idealize this role of woman as a glorified service, is an essential part of the ideology of modern industrial society.

The very structuring of the urban/suburban ecology reflects this interdependence of male work and female domestication. This means that the woman who wishes to be married and have a career must try to do both jobs at once. She must try to follow a work pattern predicated on having a female support system and provide her own support system as well as that for her husband. Because she has no wife to provide a support system for herself and can hardly do a job defined on the basis of having such a support system as well as provide her own support system and one for another person similarly employed, we must conclude that it is almost impossible for women to be married and have a career. This combination is not possible except for the rich, the manically energetic or those who manage to break out of this trap by juggling these relationships in some unorthodox way. Most women are beaten before they have even begun to fight. When the thought crosses their minds that their present portion is humanly unacceptable the odds are already hopelessly against them. We must say then that the liberation of women as a caste is impossible within the present socio-economic system. Only in a new system, a restructuring of reality in all its basic interdependencies, especially in the relationship between work time, place and the domestic support system, can women emerge into the full range of human activities presently available to the dominant class and sexual caste.

This probably means a revolutionary restructuring of society along the lines of a communitarian socialist society. State socialist societies such as Russia have collectivized much of the work of the home and thus liberated women for the male work day, but they have left the psychology of sexism in the nuclear family unchanged by still placing the fundamental burdens of housework and food procurement upon women. The communitarian socialist society on the other hand would communalize the home while keeping the basic decisions over daily life in a primary community, rather than relegating these to the state. Such a society, where many of the goods and tools of life would be produced in a workshop closely related to the primary community, is probably also the only type of society that is compatible with the long-term ecological survival of humanity because the present self-infinitizing industrial system is rapidly eating up the organic foundations of existence.[4] Many recent studies, such as Murray Bookshin's *Post-Scarcity Anarchism* and George Lakey's *Strategy for a Living Revolution*[5], have tried to delineate the scope of the present human crisis. The polarizations that lie at the heart of this crisis—the split between self and body, the split between work and pleasure, the split between city and country, farm and factory, the split that divides humans from themselves, from each other and from nature—are symbolically and socially rooted in the basic alienation between men and women. All these alienations inculcate an oppressive and domineering rather than a cooperative relation between "us" and the "other."

The communitarian socialist model cannot rule out political struggle for a socialist society on the level of national and world bodies. As Michael Harrington pointed out some years ago, modern industrialism has already created a collectivized society.[6] Classical individualist capitalism has already been destroyed by capitalism itself. The alternatives then are between democratic socialism and an elitist collectivism that benefits either political *apparatchiki*, as in the Soviet Union, or benefits a private economic elite, as in the United States. The new struggle for democracy must be a struggle to democratize systems of production and distribution that have already been collectivized on national and even international lines, to make opportunities and resources available to all persons, rather than reserving the lion's share for a small elite while leaving the masses of mankind with the crumbs. This struggle for a democratic socialist society, however, must go on at two levels; democratic distribution at the level of national and international systems and the communalization of local communities. Only when the work of the home is communalized, humanized and the immediate structures of life placed within systems of direct self-government can we hope for a society where women can participate fully in the making of society, and men can relate cooperatively to the physical foundations of their own lives. Only by rebuilding communally at the base, as well as equalizing the resources of life in the large scale systems, can we create a socialism "with a human face"; a socialism without totalitarianism.

The extent of the social revolution that is necessary not only for justice but even for survival is profoundly radical. It demands a fundamental reconstruction of the present social, economic and political systems, of which the present type of the family and its sexual interdependency are the basic foundation. Yet this revolution is insistently close at hand for it is doubtful that the present types of rapacious technology and unjust relations between rich and poor classes, sexes, races and nations can survive much longer without a world holocaust.

Because women must recognize that full justice to themselves is impossible short of a radical reconstruction of the entire system, this creates a tension between the rise of woman's consciousness and that future transformation of the world that might incarnate social justice. Theologically this hiatus corresponds to the traditional tension between baptism and final redemption—the tension between the initial conversion and incorporation into the new community and that future "New Heaven and New Earth" that overthrows the present structures of oppression and redeems the world.

Some Niebuhrians may intervene here to argue that even such a communitarian socialist society cannot represent final redemption for there must still be an ultimate redemption beyond all social structures that alone can represent redemption and that judges all social systems. This may be true, but this does not reduce the qualitative difference between social justice and social injustice. The society of social justice represents the available horizon of redemption of the world. This, from our present standpoint in the world of many kinds of oppression, represents our highest vision of a redeemed human community in a redeemed world. If it is dangerous to conflate the critical principle with a realized new society however improved, it is equally wrong not to interrelate the ultimate horizon of redemption that is beyond all imagining with that available horizon of social justice, peace and love toward which we can begin to struggle here and now. It is by divorcing ultimate salvation from the available horizon of salvation in this way and insisting that human depravity makes all social relations equally evil, that the revolutionary thrust of the Gospel is cut off and Christianity becomes an ideology of social conservativism.

Just as ultimate redemption cannot be divorced from historical redemption but must be seen as the ultimate horizon of historical redemption, so conversion cannot be privatized and internalized as something that can be completed merely by personal consciousness-raising that does not demand a transformation of the world. Redemption is not redemption from the world in a flight from outward society and nature, but redemption *of* the world, which at the same time overthrows that false world of powers and principalities that God did not create but which man creates out of his self-alienation and social exploitation. Conversion therefore cannot be fulfilled in a private inward way but must move outward toward that transformation of reality that redeems creation from bondage. This means that a tension between conversion and redemption exists as the present state of the Church; a proleptic vision and foretaste of a new world arises that also sets us in tension with the unredeemed state of our lives. Here and now our new consciousness stands as a principle of discernment and suffering conflict that struggles against the power structures in the light of a vision of redeemed humanity and creation.

The Church represents our present vantage point in this redeemed community; it is both a real foretaste of that redeemed community and the party of redemptive struggle against the power structures. It is a foretaste of redeemed humanity only in the sense of being a community of raised consciousness, not in the sense of being a community that is unaware of the many ways that alienating power structures continue to exist and our lives continue to be governed by them. From this vantage point is it possible to speak of sisterhood as the Church from the perspective of the women's movement? There are many ways in which sisterhood represents redemptive and revelatory cohumanity from the perspective of the struggle against the sexist power structure. Sisterhood is a therapeutic community that enables women to articulate their repressed alienation, to become conscious that their present portion is dehumanizing—a consciousness that all the social conditioning forces of patriarchy contrive to repress. Sisterhood gives women the basic support community to make this oppression conscious, without being delivered into loneliness and madness. Sisterhood is a healing community that makes weak women strong and able to become whole people, able to confront the sources of their debilitation with confidence. Sisterhood is also redemptive cohumanity that overcomes that internalization of self-hatred and demeaning self-images that the oppressed typically act out, not by attacking the sources of their oppression, but by attacking each other. Women in patriarchy are isolated from each other and made individually dependent on men, competitive with each other for men and prostitutes of their sexuality and domestic service for survival. Sisterhood breaks these bonds of alienation between women and restores women to redemptive cohumanity with each other.

But this provides only a base of healed selfhood from which to grapple with the real sources of debilitation in male sexism. Because the alienation between women is only a by-product of the fundamental alienation of sexism, namely the alientation between men and women, from this perspective sisterhood is inadequate to represent the Church, which must be represented by a community of both men and women of raised consciousness who see the way in which the full humanity of both men and women has been distorted by sexism. Let me make clear why this is the case. This does not mean that cohumanity can only be represented by the heterosexual married couple, as in sexist doctrines of complementarity. The Church is as much beyond heterosexist complementarity as it is beyond racism or class relationships. The Church is neither male nor female, slave nor free, Jew nor Greek; it is not a complementarity of male and female, slave and free, Jew and Greek in which each half of these alienated relationships represents a partial humanity that becomes a whole humanity. Personhood is not quantifiable in this way. The Church takes us beyond these stereotypes to that redeemed community that is possible only between whole persons.

What we mean, rather, is that the community of the oppressed against the oppressors, while it is a necessary part of the process of liberation, cannot represent the community of reconciliation. This can only be represented by a community that brings together both sides of the oppressor/oppressed relationship in a new relationship that liberates both oppressor and oppressed from their previous pathologies in relation to each other. Separatism cannot be presented as the goal of the women's movement, nor can we speak as though males alone are capable of oppressive relations while relations between "sisters" will automatically be loving. Such a view retains remnants of that Victorian feminism that regarded women as intrinsically more moral then men. To redeem humanity, therefore, one does not have to struggle against the demon in oneself. One only has to reject "evil" males and join the natural community of human goodness, namely a community of women. Such a view of women is really premoral. If women are to grow up and take responsibility for the world they must recognize that they too are capable of sin, not just as victims but as aggressors as well.[7]

In Jill Johnston's *Lesbian Nation*[8] we have a radical attempt to state a doctrine of separatism as a socio-political goal and not merely a part of the process of women's liberation. Such a view, like the similar view of black separatism from which it is borrowed, is a counsel of despair. It denies a common species-humanity underneath the separations of black and white, male and female. Such a view cannot remain neutral in separation. It entails by its very nature a rejection of the humanity of the other, a reverse sexism or racism. This does not mean that a choice of a woman's community may not be a legitimate choice as a way of working or living nonoppressively. But it is not the only choice or even a necessary choice here and now short of total reconstruction of the world. To suggest that women are "traitors" to the movement if they live with men or raise children here and now is to make two mistakes. The first is a moral absolutism that believes that there is some place of purity that can be had simply by leaving this world. It is to fail to recognize that oppression resides in each of our breasts and is structured into all the systems of life we continue to use, even if we leave the particular structure of the heterosexual marriage. Second, it makes human community between men and women either impossible by denying intrinsically the humanity of men or else something so eschatological that it is impossible to even begin to approximate it here and now. But we must affirm this community, both as a goal of ultimate liberation and as the true ground of our being that we can affirm here and now. This is not an excuse for apathy. It is an empowerment for struggle against oppressive relations that men and women can begin to work out in their life style with each other now. Any concept of liberation that simply reverses the present system of alienation and declares that the oppressor is intrinsically inhuman and reconciliation is impossible, has sold out the being of humanity upon which all liberation is based. Anger is redeeming only in the service of love, not as a fuel for destruction of the humanity of the other. In classical ethical terms one struggles against the system of oppression. One does not hate or reject the humanity of the other person who acts as the vehicle of oppression.

This does not mean that the other person is merely a passive tool of alien powers. He is a concrete beneficiary of unjust power and to that extent is guilty, responsible and still in his sins as long as the system of oppression of which he is the beneficiary continues to exist. The point is that one does not confuse nature with the fall; one does not confuse white people with the white system; one does not confuse males with the system of male domination; one does not confuse the evils that we seek to exorcise with the human beings that we seek to liberate from demonic possession. One seeks to overthrow the master as a master in order to reclaim him as a friend. One seeks to overthrow oppressive psychologies and structures to redeem a wholeness of personhood for those on each side of the alienated relationship and reveal the possibility of cohumanity for the first time. Unlike the original rise of male consciousness, the rise of women's consciousness must not translate the "other" into an object that makes him alien territory to be spurned or dominated. This process simply reverses the oppressor/oppressed relationship but leaves its psychodynamics intact. Women's consciousness, the consciousness of all oppressed people, becomes redemptive when it reveals a cohumanity beneath the master/slave distortion as the authentic ground of our being, and fights its battle in a way that takes its stand upon and constantly reaffirms this ground. Women's movements win little by simply winning new opportunities for power and practice in a world still structured by alienated consciousness. We must reach beyond this to the dissolution of both sides of every falsifying polarity and the redemption of the soul of humanity from its bondage to destruction. This is a long and difficult journey in human development. We must see this journey as one of systemic social and cultural reconstruction. Yet it is also a journey that men and women have to travel with each other. In the concluding chapter of this collection Eugene Bianchi gives an autobiographical account of what it means to one male to learn to allow his wife to be a free self-determining person and how many layers of enculturation have to be shed in order to begin that journey.

Notes: Chapter VII

1. See especially Freud's "Three Essays on Sexuality," *Complete Works*. New York: Macmillan, 1964, vol VII; See also Philips Rieff, *Freud: The Mind of the Moralist*. New York: Doubleday, 1959, chap. 5.

2. *Not in God's Image: Women in History from the Greeks to the Victorians*, Julia O'Faolain and Lauro Martines, eds. New York: Harpers, 1973, chap. VIII.6 on "Punishment," pp. 175-8.

3. Shiela Rowbotham: *A History of Women and Revolution in the Modern World*. New York: Vintage, 1972, p. 138.

4. Rosemary Ruether, "Women's Liberation, Ecology and Social Revolution," *Win* (October 4, 1973), pp. 4-7.

5. Murray Bookshin, *Post-Scarcity Anarchism*. San Francisco: Ramparts Press, 1971; George Lakey, *Strategy for a Living Revolution*. San Francisco: W. H. Freeman, 1973.

6. Michael Harrington, *The Accidental Century*, New York.: Macmillan, 1966.

7. This tendency seems to be one of the defects of Mary Daly's *Beyond God the Father*. Boston: Beacon, 1973. See review by Rosemary Ruether, *The New Republic* (November 10, 1973), pp. 24-26.

8. Jil Johnston, *Lesbian Nation*. New York: Simon & Schuster, 1973.

Chapter VIII

From Machismo to Mutuality

Eugene C. Bianchi

In previous chapters, I tried to explore the roots of the sexist development of the male psyche from an autobiographical standpoint and from the perspective of cultural conditioning in America. My personal history led me to view women as subordinates. Our social environment is immersed in aggressive male compulsions and impels us to violence. Much of what I have said has a negative tone, but such is my reading of our formative milieu. In attempting to be honest about myself and society on this vital subject I find that the reactionary and destructive dimensions of man/woman relations far outweigh the creative and positive aspects. Yet we can't afford to leave the issue with only a blunt look at past and present. We need to move ahead creatively and take tenuous personal steps towards the formation of a new male mentality and a society in which men and women can grow and share together as equal and complementary persons. This ideal serves a valuable utopian purpose when it causes us to examine the circumstances of our lives as individual men and as social beings. What are the specific areas where a variety of efforts must be made to further the humanizing/spiritualizing growth of the American male?

Before I attempt to outline some of the way-stations on the road from *machismo* to mutuality, I would like to say a word about terminology and method. *Machismo*, borrowed from Spanish-speaking lands, is a more accurate word for describing the present masculine situation than our English phrases, male chauvinist or sexist. *Macho* connotes a certain dominative and brute power; in Spanish the term signifies a kind of animal strength by which one creature controls another and thus establishes his self-identity and place in the pecking order. This aspect of domineering power for self-valuation is at the core of the male domination of women. I like the word mutuality as a general term for the goal of feminism—I would say masculinism if it were not such a clumsy mouthful—because it emphasizes interconnectedness with diversity. Androgyny might also mean such interrelatedness with difference, but it is a strange word freighted with a history of odd meanings such as the ancient hermaphrodite mixing and melding of the sexes. Mutuality for us men points towards a threefold acceptance that is denied in contemporary society. It means that we cultivate the feminine dimensions of our male selves, that we respect the diversity of homosexuality and that we come to live with women as diverse but equal others who do not exist for our aggrandizement but for our mutual growth as persons.

As for method, I will return as much as possible to the autobiographical mode. As I reflect on a number of American social institutions and mores I want to question myself and ask: What are my own attitudes, feelings and actions on this journey from *maschismo* to mutuality? This will keep me from presenting myself falsely as a kind of model feminist (masculinist?) simply because I can analyze our sexist culture in theory and talk about such high-sounding words as mutuality. No, I haven't "arrived," but I am changing. Moreover, my personal points of reference in the geography of sexist America will give others a chance to position themselves. It is all too easy for males to embrace or reject what I say as being appealing or worthless teaching. The ideas that I present remain more or less interesting "stuff out there"; they don't challenge readers to tell themselves why they feel and act a given way. Authentic growth in us takes place only when we begin from an awareness of our personalized tenets, sentiments and commitments. Otherwise our theoretical knowledge remains notional and extraneous to our developing personalities.

I begin this tour of zones where change is necessary by positioning myself on some questions relating to marriage and family. If we review the laws and customs pertaining to this basic institution it would not be difficult to demonstrate that marriage favors male rule and female subordination. Persons enter into this relationship with strong affections and a hope that things will work out. In my own case, marriage came late and we had at least theorized about roles and expectations. But the experience itself soon began to require conscious and unconscious adjustments of the contract. I would prefer to speak of marriage as an alliance or loving agreement between two persons rather than a contract, but this term has an important advantage in that it tends to spell out clearly and openly shifting mutual relationships. We have not put our contract in writing, but our unwritten agreements come up for review periodically, especially when new values are perceived or when one or the other of us backslides on responsibilities.

The tensions in our man/woman relationship revolved around three things: home chores, job/money issues and outside friendships. We have tried to divide the tasks of cooking, shopping, cleaning and the like from the beginning. This is not to say that we don't voice frustrations and resentments when the balance gets out of kilter. The very morning that I wrote these lines I found myself using an old male dodge: "But you wrap gifts so much better than I do." And I was called on it. Some may dismiss these duties as trivial, but we find them to be the stuff of everyday life that increase or lessen strains on the relationship. Women will sometimes counter that they genuinely enjoy doing all the housework or that the husband's job demands make it impossible for him to carry his share of the load. I doubt the enjoyment argument; it sounds like the rationalization of a person whose insecurities, laziness or fears keep her from confronting her man about these issues. The husband/job excuse is a serious one in that our economic system was built by men for male advantage and penalizes part-time work, both in matters of financial return and decision-making influence. But if men are truly serious about living with a woman who has enough time to develop her full potential as a partner they will have to make a twofold effort. One is to find time to do household chores in spite of their jobs; the second is to work for changes in our corporate systems that programs women into traditional housewifely roles. Many women are unfairly burdened with three jobs: housework, child-rearing and an outside job.

Professional and financial arrangements have been harder for us to reconcile than household duties. During the early years of our marriage my wife was a social worker; she is now a law student. Her experience in a public life made her more aware of her womanly potential. For feminist and other reasons she changed her name back to her birth-given name. I was both happy for her and a bit resentful of her. After all, she wasn't conforming to the styles of the typical faculty wife. I had to go to professional-social functions alone (just as she went to most of hers alone); what would my peers think of my masculinity in relation to such an "uppity" wife? I imagined them to be musing: "Poor ole Gene; he married a wild one." Then there were her professional contacts—men and women whom I didn't know but who occupied an important place in her thoughts and feelings. My attitude was a mixture of appreciation, jealousy and resentment that wavered to and fro in various indirect ways. I was glad for her, but I was also anxious about her and somewhat testy at her. An unfinished process was in operation; I was learning to exercise unused masculine emotions. Like the long-distance runner, I couldn't run the race mentally in a fieldhouse briefing; I had to feel the pain of self-change.

Attitudes and decisions about money affect a marriage in all sorts of subtle and overt ways. Two persons have different outlooks on spending and saving, on financial dependence and independence. My wife has a strong sense of a woman's need to have a clear degree of financial independence. Although we have fought over money matters, I agree that in the present social scene the reality or promise of economic independence for a woman is vital for the growth of mature male/female relations. It is not enough to reply, as men often do, that she does most of the consumer spending; this is a lame rejoinder that obscures the center of crucial decision-making. In the present structure of our world, economic power is intimately linked to major decision-making in a family. We can build up a whole network of pious ideologies about finances belonging to both of us, and that money discussion is beneath the level of our overriding love relationship. But the true test is to see how many men actually allow women to make major dispositions of family funds that can alter the whole direction and life-style of the family unit. Beyond the actual use of money, moreover, financial independence permits a woman to have a sense of options and of an authentically chosen relationship with a man. I would like to see us move towards a society that gives a woman or man a guaranteed annual income if she or he chooses full-time home and child-nurturing activities. That such a concept is so foreign to us speaks volumes about how little we really honor the role of homemaker and about the dominative place of males in money issues. My wife and I have kept our resources jointly, but we are now discussing separate accounts, at least for savings.

The most difficult dimension of our marriage focuses on the question of outside friendships. My wife's close personal friendship with a few women, as well as her participation in women's-issue groups, dramatizes the struggle to respect the full otherness of my partner. I am forced to deal with my male penchant for monopolizing the attention and concern of my wife as an expected ego-boost for the Big Man mastering the Big World. On the other side of this experience however I have discovered a new challenge for me to grow in affectional relationships with men. Not only have I drawn closer to her female friends, but I am vividly aware of the lack of similar male friendships in a culture that pushes men to relentless job achievements. The development of our friendships with persons of the opposite sex has been both an arduous and rewarding aspect of our partnership. On this score we are in no utopian situation, but our communication is clearer and more peaceful. More on this under the rubric of sexuality, below.

Perhaps the chief underlying problem that my male psyche has confronted on all these topics is the inability to listen. I mean more than merely hearing words and even comprehending their meaning. I can repeat what she said without really hearing it. Listening calls for a quality of attention and empathy for which my past hasn't educated me in reference to women. I listen for ideas and arguments, not for feelings and sensibilities. I hear the mind not the heart. My long schooling in maledom has successfully separated my head from my body; I have lived on one side of the dualism that pervades male/female relationships in western culture. We men did a first-class job of projecting body, emotion, earth and irrationality into women, and because we are numb to these dimensions within ourselves, it becomes very hard for us to listen to anyone, especially to women whom we have always assumed to be lesser humans.

Men need to think about motherhood and child-rearing practices if we desire to foster better family relationships. Before I pontificate on this subject, I should acknowledge that we do not now have children. Yet our choice in a five-year-old marriage to postpone having children arises from serious thought about the demands of parenting and child-rearing. The element of genuine choice is uppermost in this matter. The accidental and unwanted child often suffers in an environment of semirejection and resentment, although some people adjust reasonably well to unexpected children. Yet men in our culture do not take seriously the burdens and responsibilities of parenting. Their role is usually reduced to provider and occasional playmate for the kids. Men wax eloquent about the glories of motherhood, but how many of them would exchange their jobs for the full-time demands of child care? Woman's work, man's work . . . our categories are set in ways that confine women to the world of minors so that we can be free to expand in an adult world. We manufacture all sorts of guilt-producing theories for women who take on careers when they are mothers of young children. If women work we expect them to carry the double weight of housework as well. But we do not press to alter the socio-economic system so that fathers can assume half of child care, nor are we solicitous about changing national policy so that resources will be allocated for excellent day care. The system serves us well; it is geared to liberating men for ego-enhancing activities.

There is a great need in our country for quality day-care centers. Eight million children from deprived families are in desperate need of such facilities, but millions of other families could also benefit greatly by having such institutions available for their children. It would foster the mental, physical and social development of children while allowing parents to have other options for their talents. Admittedly, I agree with those specialists who hold that the quality of parental time spent with the young is more valuable than sheer quantity, but the main root of opposition to comprehensive day care is the male psyche that sees this development as disturbing on at least two levels. First, it would free women for threatening job competition and it would give them a kind of independence in the world that menaces male control of the female life-style. Second, President Nixon's veto of the Comprehensive Child Development Act disclosed an underlying fear of good day care as a socializing mode of educating children. Nixon's suspicions are accurate; at issue here is the possibility of upsetting the fundamental pattern of isolated, nuclear family formation of children in the mold of the individualistic competitive model. Thus a network of subsidized child-care centers is rejected while hundreds of millions of dollars are wasted in military cost overruns.

Amid the problems of human sexuality I single out for special male consideration two crucial and interrelated facets: equality and relationship. In other words, the context of our sexual life as men is one of dealing with an inferior in a performance/act manner. The culture teaches us in manifold ways that men are superior, and it schools us to understand this superiority in terms of achievement-oriented deeds. Authentic love, on the other hand, as the basis for rewarding sex is impossible without equality of persons who communicate in a full relationship. Such a theoretical framework helps me to understand my own sexual inadequacies. Although I would have protested that I viewed the main woman in my life as an equal, I found it very difficult to let her be free to decide about her own relationships with other men. I would like to stress, however, that the open marriage theory on the possibility and even desireability of extra-marital sexual relations can be both deceptive and destructive. It is deceptive in that its main argument can easily cover over serious affectional problems in the marriage that are allowed to go unheeded. The thesis runs something like this: we can't be everything to each other; therefore, outside sex will complement the primary relationship. Such a rationale for extra-marital sex is enticing, but it often becomes a smoke screen that prevents husband and wife from dealing in depth with their own intimacy problems. The result can be disastrous for the primary relationship. My own conviction is that the overwhelming majority of married people cannot cope creatively with extra-marital sex. This dimension of sexual liberation is beguiling but full of pitfalls. I wouldn't normally deal with an equal on the basis of jealousy and possessiveness. When I got in touch with the fears and insensitivities. Homosexuality elicits revulsion based on fear in cept her need for freedom. A sexual double standard has been the traditional sign of the subordination of the female. None of these changes can be realized without pain and risk, nor am I without feelings of anger, possessiveness and jealousy. But I'm not as controlled by them as I was, and our sexuality as the experience of equals has matured. When the act/performance orientation that influences my sexual conduct lessens, the possibility for sexual relationship increases. The latter goes beyond contact with a subordinate as an object of gratification to reach a complex of attention and affection that unifies two persons.

Our attitudes on sexuality as men will have to be exorcised of other fears and insensitivities. Homosexuality elicits revulsion based on fear in many men. We are insecure about our own masculinity in a culture that demands performance according to a *macho* set of rules. Out of our terror at the prospect of finding male-oriented affections in ourselves, we lash out at homophiles. Nearly all of the institutions I've known have taught me to suppress emotional expression toward men. I now seriously challenge such sexual "marinating." I want to accept homosexuals as persons with a different sexual orientation, and I hope to be able to express warmth and feeling towards men in ways that are right for me. Our insensitivity toward women is also shown in our disregard for the risks we impose on them concerning contraception and abortion. It will be interesting to notice how males react when they face taking a birth control pill every day

—with its possible side effects. Nor do we truly sense the pain and apprehension of women who confront an unwanted pregnancy; because it doesn't happen in our bodies we can easily approve or condemn abortion with principled abstractions.

If we intend to move to a society of mutuality, education of boys and young men will require serious revision. Home and school alone can't bring about the needed changes, but they can be important starting points. The most significant education of the young in the earliest years will result from the modeling of parental relations. How much does sexism pervade father/mother interactions as well as those with friends? Will boys learn to compete fiercely in sport and school in order to gain parental respect and their own self-esteem? Will they learn early that gun, bat and car are extensions of virility, of the manly power to dominate, win, make it? Then there is the lock-step regimentation of the schools to train boys uncritically for expected male behavior. Will the patterns of our educational factories that mill young men into insensitive professional elites be broken and humanized? Faculty men can encourage women students to develop confidence in their talents and enter many fields previously closed to them. Faculties and administrations can integrate themselves sexually by hiring more women at all levels.

As we move to the wider social realm in our search for directions to mutuality, it may appear that the structures of *machismo* are impossible to modify. Older men are said to be set in their ways and protective of vested interests. Yet from my own experience I find that many men in middle and later years are unsatisfied with doing what they were programed to do. In many ways discontent with life-style patterns is stronger in men of forty than in the college students I teach. The challenge is to discover creative and gratifying channels to release this potential for social and personal change among men. In science, business and the professions men can raise their awareness of oppressive masculine patterns that prevent a fuller life for women and stymie growth in humanness for men.

The opening of many previously interdicted occupations to women is in large measure the responsibility of men in positions of influence in union and management. The prospect of inflation and unemployment can't be solved by discriminating against minorities or majorities such as women. The trend towards more women in law and medical schools is hopeful, but a great amount of work still needs to be done by lawyers and judges to rescind anti-female legislation that is still on the books in many states. Property, consumer and welfare laws are a few areas where there is discrimination against women. The Equal Rights Amendment, now only a half dozen states from ratification, will be an important equalizing opportunity. But again it is mostly men who hold the destiny of ERA in their hands, and for the foreseeable future, male legislators and judges will be in positions to place obstacles to its implementation. We know how dogged such resistance can be when we remember that this is the twentieth year since the Supreme Court's integration decision.

The churches as male-regulated institutions have a special responsibility to lead the way for women's rights. Because churches and synagogues see themselves as the sensitive consciences of society they should be moved to an extraordinary commitment for justice and equality out of both repentance and zeal. Men in the churches could find ample material for repentance by reflecting on the centuries of subtle and manifest discrimination against women. Not only did the churches propagate subjugating stereotypes with theological ideology from within but, as a major influence in Western culture, Christianity fostered the given male/female roles in society at large. I find that religious studies in higher education are a fine medium for exploring the historical and doctrinal dimensions of masculine religiousness. But in most ecclesiastical institutions the task of opening all levels of churchly life to the full participation of women has scarcely begun. The problem of those who have power in the churches clinging to it is also common to other social institutions. But a special element of hypocrisy enters into the picture for churches because humble service and sharing, not dominative power, is its proclaimed ideal.

The communications media, especially television, bear a heavy responsibility for the continuance of *machismo* in America. Again the media are directed by men who bolster their self-image and enrich themselves with shows and advertisements that inculcate the stereotypes by which the vast majority of people live. That women are bought by the industry to sell the stereotypes to other girls and women is not surprising. Blacks sold blacks into slavery for money; for a good deal more money, Superflys and Shafts sell fellow blacks into a new slavery of *macho* values. Like oppressed groups before them, many women on the screen and in the audience have so internalized their oppression that they identify it with true femininity. But at the end of all these stories, white men make the big profits and decisions. Protest within the media is dangerous; jobs and futures are at stake. But how aware are the viewers that they are being taken, and where are the organized consumer efforts to protest the insults against feminine humanity? If there was ever an agency that should belong to all the people, and not to a few profiteers, it is television. But such is not the reality in the United States. I will suspect that things are starting to change when I see a detergent or a floor wax being sold to a man or when a panel of male corporation executives attests to the wonders of a particular toilet bowl cleaner used by them after a board meeting.

We could proceed to examine other social institutions in which men can take steps from *machismo* to mutuality. The nuances would shift, but the basic patterns for change would remain the same. The questioning of stereotypes, the challenging of attitudes and the creation of new perspectives and actions could repeat itself into banality. Yet it is precisely the prosaic dimension of this social revolution that we must be willing to embrace. A culture of mutuality will not be formed in a moment or a year by some grand exploit or by a charismatic leader. It is the small gains in many places at once that will almost imperceptibly lever us out of a chauvinist culture and into a new era of possibilities. This is how the chief images according to which I modeled my own life changed from period to period. Before I was even aware of the shift in thought and commitment the old paradigms had been discarded. The most important revolutions happen in our guts and feelings before they enter consciousness. So will it be with the quest for mutuality.

At this point, it would be well to clarify and discuss an underlying premise of all my remarks. What assurance do I have that if men change along the lines prescribed and women achieve a parity of relationships they will be any more humane? Won't power corrupt women as it has men? Will females be any less competitive, avaricious and brutal than men? What benefit will come to society by these alterations? I have no assurance that these negative results will not indeed happen. I have only a strong hope enveloping a guiding insight. (They couldn't do much worse than men in directing our fortunes; why not give them a chance? But this is no answer to the questions.) I believe that through many centuries of socialization the qualities of compassion, intuition, cooperation and a unifying acceptance of nature and people have been far more cultivated among women. These feminine dimensions are latent but stunted in most men today, especially among those who rise to commanding positions where toughness is paramount. The core of my hope stems from the fact that women have been closer to the sources of life, to the wisdom of earth, to the pain and the value of birthing. Women know in a special way that life is precious and precarious. I trust that these qualities will counterbalance our male proclivities to follow only that part of ourselves bent on ego-building through domination and achievement. "And a child shall lead them." Like Fellini, my child is a girl.

Yet even if we admit that women could make special and needed contributions to humanizing our institutions, men will tend to see this development as a loss to themselves. The threats to masculinity, status and power will not be easy to resolve after years of conditioning. A first phase in the re-education of the male psyche would consist in the overcoming of false myths about women that still pervade our thinking. These myths are useful tools for maintaining the status quo and warding off the anxieties of change. Here is a list of cherished male images with a brief rejoinder to each. Women are weaker and irrationally emotional. But they could be stronger; they already have more endurance, and the emotionality charge is ill-founded. Women have already made great progress toward their goals. But the statistics since the 1930s show a decline of women in the professions; they haven't "come a long way, baby." Women lose more work time. Again the facts show that this is not true. Children and the family will suffer. Yet the very opposite may and does actually happen; this unwarranted belief needs more investigation as we turn to a second phase in re-orienting the male mentality.

Men need to ponder the values to themselves that could result from supporting the goals of the women's movement. I find myself freer in an adult relationship with my feminist wife. Although I cherish our relationship as primary, I can relate without guilts and worries to other friends, men and women. On this matter much more could be said about honest communication, but it would draw us too far afield. In general, however, I believe that a man can have a more honest relationship with a woman who is self-confident and self-sufficient. Indirection, cunning and deviousness are not necessary. Another rewarding aspect of living with a woman who is developing many sides of herself is the number of things that we can share with one another. Although it isn't always true, the woman whose life is confined to the home tends to be provincial and petty in her scope. I would suppose too that men could get closer to their children if they were seen as the full responsibility of both parents.

Besides these personal advantages to men, social rewards should also be considered. I realize that all our economic provisions do not depend on my work alone. Because I care about my job for other than financial reasons I probably work at it with the same intensity as if all the money responsibilities rested on my shoulders. But the money pressure is less; I can stay with a job that I like more even though it pays less. Quantifying intense competition, in the classic American mode, gives way to a kind of competition with myself about quality and commitments, although I'm still far from having integrated that goal into myself. I also experience an increase in my freedom to take public stands, criticize the educational institution and possibly even quit it. If I were a divorced man I would relish the prospect of freedom from alimony and total child support.

In most of the foregoing I have not used theological language, yet in my understanding of religiousness and Christianity the theological dimension is inextricably joined to the human. The use of traditional religious terms can give the illusion of spirituality, but if these words do not proceed from the joy and the pain, the challenge and the promise of everyday personal and social existence they lack substance. To travel from *machismo* to mutuality in this culture we men need to grapple with the concrete issues and attitudes that continue to determine our self-identity and self-worth. For me, this means a struggle against the self-deception that tells me that I can leap quickly to the new life of mutuality by thinking and mouthing pious phrases. It means resisting the self-deception of believing that the civilization around me will rapidly change its age-old indoctrinations. It is only when I can taste the brokenness of my own finitude and experience the resisting weight of oppression in society that I may be on the verge of the conversion leading to liberation.

This conversion or *metanoia* is an overlapping and recurring process that gradually releases me from male bondage and opens me to the possibility of cohumanity. It is a process of unlearning what it signifies to be a man according to the masculine formula that I have inherited from my forebears since the beginning of recorded history. It is an awesome challenge. I want to be freed from that self-valuation based on the traits of domineering power: toughness, competition, rational insensitivity and the superiority that excludes others from touching my life. Such conversion is at the heart of the Gospels; it is that continual grace that calls us away from the bondage of manipulating others in the perverted desire to enlarge and secure the self. This "law of sin and death" hovers over our lives and our institutions. In man/woman relations I engage in struggle for self and societal liberation at the deepest level. For what is at stake is more than professional reputation or social acceptance; my very humanness as a man/person is at issue. My very soul, my religiousness, is at stake, for how can I be open to the Spirit of God, if I am closed off in the circle of sexual oppressions?

Yet the path from *machismo* to mutuality in myself is not only a liberation *from* an alienating sexism; it is also a freeing *for* new styles of relationship. As we approach mutuality, we will go beyond the abstraction of looking at men and women as full persons. It is too facile to say in a conceptual and universal way that we are all equal. Although such generalities are true, there is a more costly and precious freedom in being able to accept and respect the concrete otherness of the other. Just as I need to embrace my own particularity as this man freed from past stereotypes, so too I must learn to accept woman not only as a fellow human but as a distinct and different individual.

This degree of liberation will demand dialogue and vulnerability. Although the separateness of men's and women's liberation groups has a valuable function, the conversation between aware men and women on the requirements of mutuality must not be broken. Ruether argues this point well in her discussion of sisterhood (Chapter III). Amid the misunderstandings and failures on this journey I must also risk being vulnerable to the other. In the end, the process of my liberation demands that I relinquish total self-sufficiency and allow myself to be criticized and helped by the other. Without this trust there will be no freeing of self. As we allow ourselves to become more vulnerable, that is more sensitive as men to the personal and social issues that I've outlined on the pilgrimage from *machismo* to mutuality, we will eventually build a society where brothers and sisters can be free to experience together the full potential of their humanity.

Epilogue: New Beginnings

Rosemary Ruether

In the early 1960s it was common among American Catholics to speak with enthusiasm of the two John's—John Kennedy and Pope John XXIII. Strange though it may seem to make twins of an elderly Italian pope and a young, rich and not very religious American President of Irish descent, the two Johns symbolized for American Catholics two points in a new consciousness and self-confidence. As Americans and as Catholics they felt they had come of age, emerged out of the political ghetto of second-class citizenship in WASP America and out of the spiritual ghetto of a Counter-Reformation Catholicism that had turned its back upon modern history. American Catholics had joined the main stream of society politically and intellectually, perhaps even had become pacesetters. I remember when Pope John's encyclical letter *Pacem in Terris* appeared in 1963. The *Los Angeles Times* carried a banner headline crying POPE JOHN'S LETTER TO US! When had the non-Catholic world before displayed such interest and respect for things Catholic, even identifying themselves as the recipients of a bounty of grace from the pope? There was a brief period, perhaps three or four years, which we now recognize only in retrospect, when American Catholics were almost like a people intoxicated with the sudden expansion of their world. The doors on an expanding horizon had swung open and we rediscovered the dimension of the future as redemptive possibility. Ancient problems seemed to be on the brink of solution in a new Enlightenment. The bitter taint of racism of a nation born half slave and half free could be dispelled. The pockets of poverty marring the uniform affluence of the land would yield to the social engineering of the "best and the brightest" whom the handsome young president brought with him from the elite reserve banks of genius.

The Church too had a few problems that needed clearing up. It was a bit backward in its notions of marriage and sexuality. It was out of step with modern democratic methods of management. There might even be a theological problem here and there that needed a bit of redefining. But mostly, like good pragmatists, we thought of the Church's problems in terms of updating its organization and practice. Things like exegesis, systematic theology and Church history were arcane enterprises only tangentially related to the issues of modernization. Most of all we were sure that we were the Church. It was up to us, the pundits of lay journalism, to decide these things. The august bishops of Vatican II had told us so, we believed.

As the early Sixties gave way to the late Sixties the shadows lengthened over this optimism until they all but closed off that bright confidence of those hopeful days. First one Kennedy and then a second was hurled at our feet, spattered with his own blood, as was Martin Luther King. The cities burned. The toll of assassinations and shattered expectations mounted. The best and the brightest revealed themselves as the engineers of Vietnam, counter-insurgency abroad and paranoia and repression at home. Kennedy was followed by Johnson, who was followed by Nixon.

In the Church too the eclat of the simple pope who trusted people gave way to the scholar-diplomat filled with fears and dire warnings. The bishops, now back in their dioceses, discovered with shock what they had been led to say in Rome and now made haste to retrench their powers. Evasion, manipulation and a taste here and there of a good old inquisition whittled our hopes down to cynicism.

All in vain? No. We have too easily forgotten what we were like before that turbulent decade. We suffer if anything from having done and learned so much so fast. We were engulfed in an escalation of consciousness. Our minds and energies rushed from one expanding vista to the next, discovering ever new dimensions to the problems of bigotry, injustice and systemic oppression until finally what began with a few Jim Crow laws in the southern United States encompassed the entire globe. Our natural ecology itself, the very earth under our feet and the air we breathed, became the framework that gathered up the earth and all our history into a structure of destruction. What use the fight with paltry weapons of the Movement? The broken-down mineo machine, the walk-up office in the poorest part of town, the small circle of bright and marginal intellectuals whose company had once so intoxicated us? The Kent State massacre began the great drop-out of the college generation and a stampede of disillusioned youth began back to disappointed affluence and retreat into a private world of security and personal experience. The greening of America, like the greening of Hiroshima, became a rampant jungle-like antigrowth arising from a blasted landscape of the soul.

Are we ready for a new evaluation, a new, steadier, but longer, deeper look at our past, our possibilities, the deep set of the evil of our ways formed by history, yet still reclaiming a basic covenant with God and humanity in the Church, of people with each other in the nation upon which We the People can stand, upon which we can rebuild foundations for a different future? For those of us who have not run away from the problems of social justice, problems that have become identical with human survival, the Seventies must succeed the Sixties, not as a time of disillusionment, but as the time of deeper reflection with much more fundamental spadework into the archeology of our dilemma, charting its roots and causes in the total structure of our distorted social selfhood, in order to envision the ecology of an entirely new environment.

It is in this mood of deeper reflection that it may be that sexism becomes the issue of the Seventies as racism was the issue of the Sixties, not to brush aside or replace the consciousness of racial oppression, but to find the even more deeply buried root of that need to repress the dark part of our selves and to project it upon victimized peoples. As racism showed us the visible socio-economic dimension of oppression, sexism reveals the psychopathology of oppression. Sexism takes us to the inner split in the self, the mechanisms of self-alienation involved in making other peoples a subordinate and auxiliary humanity to a male ruling class. It reveals not only the distortions that must go on in the psyches and social conditioning of oppressed people to shape them to be servant and shadow selves of rulers but also to show the distortions that must go on in the ruling group themselves, who must repress their own more empathic and intuitive capacities to shape themselves into domineering egoism. It is to be hoped that this little collection of essays will make a special contribution to this analysis because it brings together in tandem the reflections both of a woman on the distortions of woman's being as a result of sexism and the reflection of a man on the distortions of male being through sexism.

These essays also hoped to combine reflections on both the American scene and the Church, especially the Catholic Church, the tradition of the authors. As Americans and as Christians we inherit a political and a spiritual revolutionary tradition from which we draw the principles of our criticism of oppression and exploitation. Yet we also inherit a betrayal of those revolutions by the governments and church organizations who claim to represent those traditions. We wish to sell short neither side of this dramatic dialectic. We do not wish to minimize the depths of the betrayal that is involved in a Church that started by proclaiming the redemption of all humanity from mutual hostility and yet soon found ways to degrade women to second-class citizenship and failed to oppose a slave society. The author of the Epistle to the Ephesians, who ratified a subjection of wives to husbands modeled on the subjugation of the creature to God, established a sexist idolatry in the heart of Christian symbolism that allowed males to play God in relation to subjugated women. (Eph. 5:21-24). Similarly, the instruction to slaves to "be obedient to those who are your earthly masters with fear and trembling as to Christ" (Eph. 6:5) established an idolatrous identification of the *dominus* as both husband and slave master with Christ, an identification that is evident in the medieval Christian use of the word Lord in all three senses. Such statements failed to understand the radical message of the Gospel that "in Christ there is neither Jew nor Greek, slave nor free, male nor female (Gal. 3:23) that the author of Ephesians alludes to only a few chapters earlier when he declares that in Christ we have been made one, breaking down the walls of hostility of those alienated from each other. (Eph. 2:14-16). This betrayal of the heart of the Gospel began in the earliest Church, which was not able to appropriate the radical proclamation of reconciliation and freedom and apply it to the socially oppressive structures of the inherited order. The betrayal grew apace, affiliating the Church repeatedly with the powers and principalities of Caesar until for most people it is now difficult to recognize the Church as a paradigm of a liberated humanity in any sense.

In our American Revolution, idolatry was hidden in the heart of our proclamations of freedom and equality. That universal humanity in whose name all "men" were declared equal turned out to be made in the image of the male white Protestant ruling class. Neither slaves nor Indians were considered human in the sense of being able to claim these rights of humanity and citizenship. Even Irish and Eastern and Southern European Catholics and Jews departed sufficiently from the norm to find it necessary to struggle against an initiation into second-class citizenship. Most of all it is that female part of the human race whose independent humanity is denied by that confusion of the male with generic humanity.

On March 31, 1776, Abigail Adams wrote to her husband, John

Adams, then attending the Continental Congress in Philadelphia, claiming for women those rights of humanity being declared in the name of "all men":

> In the new code of laws which I suppose it will be necessary for you to make, I desire you would remember the ladies and be more generous and favorable to them than your ancestors. Do not put such unlimited power into the hands of the husbands. Remember that all men would be tyrants if they could . . . That your sex are naturally tyrannical is a truth so thoroughly established as to admit of no dispute, but such of you as wish to be happy willingly give up the harsh title of master for the more tender and endearing one of friend. Why then not put it out of the power of the vicious and the lawless to use us with cruelty and indignity with impunity. Men of sense of all ages abhor those customs which treat us only as vassals of your sex.

With a vigor that was only gradually to emerge in American women, Abigail Adams appropriated the spirit of the American Revolution itself to proclaim women in no way beholden to those laws that would continue to define them as servants and property of their husbands, objects even of their brutality with impunity:

> If particular care and attention is not paid to the ladies, we are determined to forment a rebellion and will not hold ourselves bound by any laws in which we have no voice or representation.

John Adams' reply to this appeal reveals how far from the minds of the Founding Fathers it was to consider not only women but various other categories of subject people in those rights of men then being proclaimed.

> As to your extraordinary code of laws, I cannot but laugh. We have been told that our struggle has loosened the bonds of government everywhere; that children and apprentices were disobedient; that schools and colleges were grown turbulent; that Indians slighted their guardians and Negroes grew insolent to their masters. But your letter was the first intimation that another tribe, more numerous and powerful than all the rest, were grown discontented.

A bloody Civil War, the rending of the nation by racial strife, the genocide of the native Americans and a hundred-year struggle by women to earn the right to vote were only some of the outcomes of the inability of the Founding Fathers to take their own words of equality and justice seriously.

American society in its short two-hundred year history has seen continual struggles to extend that definition of citizenship and to make good the promise of a society of equality and justice for all that was betrayed by the ruling race, class and sexual caste. The Christian Church in its two thousand year history has also been rent by continual struggles for reform and renewal. The turbulent histories of both these traditions are rooted in the contradiction between the revolutionary principles of their foundation and the betrayal of these principles to established structures of power. In this sense, the reformers rightly claim to be standing on the principles of the original covenants and seeking to uncover those principles again in their radical purity and to refound each community anew in the image of that original vision. Thus Americanism, not accidently, through both its Puritan and its Enlightenment origins, has about it something of the dialectical movement of the Gospel. Its own foundations transcend its historical actuality, constantly leading it out into a new future. The principles of its foundation do not stand behind it, sanctifying the status quo of a past order. But these principles are constantly in exodus ahead of the reality of these communities, challenging the validity of the present order and holding up the vision of a community of justice, a community of redemption, a peaceable kingdom of prophetic hope.

Does it seem inappropriate and even blasphemous to compare an American gospel and a Christian Gospel in this way? I think not. To do so would be idolatry if the hopes of the Christian Gospel were identified with the American reality. But then the hopes of the Christian Gospel become idolatry when they are identified with the Christian reality as well. Idolatry consists of absolutizing the status quo in the name of a visionary hope. Both American hope and Christian hope have an alternative possibility, a prophetic tension that makes the hope of their own covenants a continual source of tension and restlessness. The hopes and commandments of both the Christian covenant and the American covenant work constantly to delegitimize the actuality of these historical communities in order to stir them again into a new exodus in search of that liberated community that is the mandate for their existence. In this sense, American hope, like the hopes of many other revolutionary peoples, can be seen as the historical dimension of the Gospel that prophetically challenges our established reality and calls us to transcend ourselves towards that authentic humanity of the future whose final horizon is the Kingdom of God. Political hope and biblical hope are not two separate and noncommunicating streams. Both refer to the one humanity created by one God whose mandate for creation is redemption and whose commandment is to build a world where the reign of powers and principalities has been broken and all things have become "very good."

Rosemary Radford Ruether
Washington, D.C.
August 1974

Reflection and Discussion

Chapter I

1. Discuss the relationship of nature and culture in the formation of the images of "masculine" and "feminine."

2. What ideas and qualities do you associate with men; what ones with women; what ones with humanity? How are the first two related to the third?

3. What qualities and images do you associate with God the Father? How would this be changed if you thought of God as mother? As friend?

Chapter II

1. What were the formative influences—persons, institutions, events— that shaped your understanding of being man or woman and of how the sexes were expected to think and act?

2. How do you judge the values and failures of your particular masculine or feminine upbringing and education?

3. From your own experience as a man or woman, what needs to be changed in your life in order to become a more complete male or female person?

Chapter III

1. What seems to be the relationship between secularization, the privatization of religion and the changing image of women according to this essay? Can you illustrate this relationship from your own experience?

2. The author shows that industrialization changed the economic role of the home. How does this affect the image and role of women? Can you illustrate this from your own experience?

3. The author speaks of the double image of women in Western ideology: the good, virginal woman and the bad, carnal woman. She suggests that this split image tended to be identified with upper- and lower-class women and white and black women in class and racist societies. How would you illustrate this from your own experience?

Chapter IV

1. What did you learn over the years (and from whom) about masculine and feminine ways of dealing with human aggression?

2. Can you identify with, or dispute or add to, what the author says about the relationship of violence and social institutions such as family, school, peer group and athletics?

3. Do you think that the masculine mystique is violence-prone in reference to both American crime and to economic and political institutions?

Chapter V

1. Discuss from your own training the meaning of the word "love" and the meaning of "sex," as you were taught to understand them. How

were they supposed to be different? How were they supposed to be related? Do you feel there is a necessary conflict between the two? Why?

2. Do you feel that homosexuality is "natural" or "unnatural"? What are your reasons for taking one or the other viewpoint? Does sex/love between men seem different to you than sex/love between women? Why?

3. What does sexual liberation mean to you? What does women's liberation mean to you? How are they related? How are they different?

Chapter VI

1. What would you cite in your own experience that confirms or questions the author's understanding of psychic celibacy?

2. Have you been taught to act according to the traditional masculine or feminine traits described in the essay? If so, which ones?

3. As a man or a woman what qualities do you believe should be fostered in your personality, and what concrete steps can you take in that direction?

Chapter VII

1. How were you taught to understand the meaning of sin and the fall of man? How does this seem different from the way the author is using these words?

2. How were you taught to understand the meaning of redemption and the Church? How does this seem different from the way the author is using these words?

3. How would you envision the organization of society that would allow women and men to actualize their talents, intelligence and leadership abilities equally, especially the relationship between the functions now associated with the family and the home and the functions associated with work and the public world?

Chapter VIII

1. If you are a man, what specific steps have you taken (or might you take) in relationships with women or other men that could move you from *machismo* to mutuality?

2. If you are a woman, what are the attitudes and actions that you would like to see men, in general, and especially those closest to you, cultivate?

3. Can you project in imagination your own ideal social order in which men and women would interact in more equal and humane ways? To achieve this state or approximate it, how would social and cultural institutions have to change?